FLASHING LIGHTS NOT INCLUDED.
The 1992 Grand Prix GTP. Official Pace Car Of NASCAR 21 Years Running.

We're proud of our long association with NASCAR. And we're equally proud to offer the serious driving enthusiast one of the most exciting Pontiacs ever. The 1992 Grand Prix™ GTP. Its specs are impressive. A 210 hp 24-valve V6 engine. Computer-controlled anti-lock brakes. 16-inch high-performance Goodyear Eagle ZR50 tires. A sport-tuned, fully independent suspension. A cockpit purposefully designed and equipped to serve the most demanding agenda. All packaged in a shape sleek enough to race <u>and</u> pace NASCAR. Trust us. The new Pontiac Grand Prix GTP will set the pace on any street. Even without flashing lights.

PONTIAC MOTORSPORTS. We Build Excitement.

The most successful te

He didn't just win here once. He did it seven times.
It's a record that may never be broken.
Richard Petty truly is the King of Racing.
We couldn't be prouder to have been his partner for 21 years.
And that he's been using STP® Oil Treatment since 1972 to help him win.

am in Daytona history.

All good things must come to an end, though. Richard has announced that this will be his last season as a driver on the NASCAR circuit.

We'll miss seeing number 43 on the starting line. 21 years is a long time. But it went by very fast.

STP. The edge.

See the 1992 Fan Appreciation Tour, a salute to the fans from Richard Petty and STP. It's coming to all NASCAR races this season.

CONTENTS

PUBLISHED BY: Autosport International, Inc.
PUBLISHER: John Norwood
ASSOCIATE PUBLISHER: Barbara Hassler-Steig
ART DIRECTOR: Robert Steig
EDITOR: Jonathan Hughes
FRONT COVER PHOTOGRAPHY: Daytona International Speedway
BACK COVER PHOTOGRAPHY: Steve Swope

PHOTOGRAPHIC TEAM: Dan Bianchi, Michael C. Brown, Linda McQueeney, Ron McQueeney, Steve Swope, and the photographic staff of Daytona International Speedway, headed by Bob Constanzo.

SPEED LIVE

SPEED WEEKS 1992

Daytona International Speedway President Jim Foster surveys the packed stands and bustling infield captured in the photographer's fisheye lens.

Daytona International Speedway

ROLEX 24 AT DAYTONA

NISSAN WINS AT RECORD SPEED, TOPPLING JAGUAR AND PORSCHE ROUSH MUSTANGS MAKE IT 8 IN A ROW IN GTS

A Toyota was on the pole but Nissans led virtually every lap in the newly minted Rolex 24 at Daytona, North America's premiere endurance race. A normally aspirated 3.5 liter V8 car in "LeMans" trim, driven by an all-Japanese team took the checkered flag at a new record average speed of 112.897 mph. Masahiro Hasemi, the '91 Japanese touring car champion, Kazuyoshi Hoshino, and Toshio Suzuki piloted the car flawlessly, posting fastest race lap along the way (1:38.495). Prior to Speed Weeks they had never seen the Daytona circuit. Davy Jones, David Brabham ('91 IMSA Champion Geoff's younger brother), and a pair of Scotts, IndyCar drivers Goodyear and Pruett, took a solid second place in a big 6.5 liter Jaguar V12, albeit nine laps in arrears. Ironically, Jaguar is credited with the IMSA GTP winner's points and Nissan is left out in the cold, since LeMans-type (Group C) cars can take the cash and the glory but aren't eligible for points. Nissan's IMSA points-eligible cars succumbed, one to an accident, the other to a blown engine. Hurley Haywood, leading the Team 0123 Porsche 962 entry which finished third overall, couldn't believe that the flying Nissans would last. Nor could teammate Eje Elgh, a Swede, who, with Austrian Roland Ratzenberger and Indy-Car driver Scott Brayton completed the team. Instead, it was their Porsche which suffered mechanical gremlins, a broken brake caliper late in the proceedings, which cost the team four

laps and a shot at top GTP honors. The misfortune did not, however, keep them off the victory podium, a tradition established by Porsche for placing in the top three in every IMSA 24 hours at the Daytona venue.

With Nissan so comfortably out in front overall, much of the spectator interest shifted to the grand touring cars. Not one to disappoint spectators or his backers back in Dearborn, Whistler Mustang team owner Jack Roush directed his 8th straight win for Ford Motor Co. pony cars. (The old GTO category is now called GTS.) Drivers Wally Dallenbach Jr., Robby Gordon, and Dorsey Schroeder were so far ahead with three hours to go that they could afford to park their racer and win on accumulated mileage. Park it they did, an hour later, with engine maladies, content to spruce up the Mustang for victory circle. A Rocketsports Olds Cutlass driven by Paul Gentilozzi, Darin Brassfield, George Robinson, and Jeff Kline was second in GTS, albeit 24 laps in arrears. Early in the proceedings, the second Roush Mustang suffered the indignity of a severe tangle with the guard rail, while NASCAR driver Mark Martin was at the wheel. Co-drivers Calvin Fish and Jim Stevens hustled out to the scene with a mixed bag of spares and made repairs, (Only drivers are allowed to work on the car on the circuit.) and got the car back to the pits. Five hours later the trio plus co-driver Robbie Buhl were back in the fray and, at the end, were rewarded with third place for

their industry. In the GTU category, Mazda once again reigned supreme, notching the make's 11th victory in a row. Drivers were Dick Greer, Al Bacon, Peter Uria, and Mike Mees. The victory was a repeat for Greer, the car owner as well as driver, and Mees. A Mazda was second in the category, too, this one an MX6 piloted by Eduardo and Juan Dibos plus cousin Raul Orlandini.

The Bob Leitzinger, Butch Leitzinger, David Loring and Chuck Kurtz driving team brought a Nissan 240 SX home third, after setting a new record in qualifying.

In the Camel Lights division, the Comptech Acura of Parker Johnstone, Dan Marvin, Jim Vasser, and Steve Cameron provided a rerun of the team's '91 victory, out of the lead only a handful of laps, none of which was the all-important one at the 24 hour mark. A handsome fifth place overall was the payoff for a fast consistent, error-free performance. The Buick powered Kudzu of Andy Evans, Fermin Velez, Lon Bender and Dominic Dobson was fast, but only fast enough for second place in the category.

As can happen in an endurance contest, the overall winner, and the category winners, were so far ahead in the countdown hours that it was purely a matter of running out the clock. Speaking of time pieces, the winners received Rolex watches presented personally by Rolex Watch U.S.A. President Roland Puton.

"The difference between this and other

The Rolex 24 at Daytona.

It is a race like none other in America. A place where names like Foyt and Gurney are legend. The ultimate proving ground where for 24 straight hours they battle the road, the fatigue, the elements, and each other. This is not just another Sunday afternoon at the track. This is where exotic V-12s duel with full-bore V-8s in the heat of the day and through the solid black wall of night.

Then it starts to rain.

But the true storms at The Daytona International Speedway have raged not in the skies, but down on the track. In 1962, after his engine failed, Dan Gurney nursed his winning Lotus across the line on the power of his starter motor, much to the crowd's delight. The mid-sixties saw classic duels between Ford and Ferrari, with Ford's prototypes puncturing Ferrari's domination with wins in 1965 and 1966, only to have Ferrari's 330 P4s come back for revenge in 1967. And then it was Porsche's turn, with drivers like Peter Gregg and Hurley Haywood dominating the next two decades at Daytona.

Hurley Haywood has his name engraved a record five times on the Rolex Cup.

Dan Gurney awaits the checkered flag in 1962.

This is the full-horsepower legend of Daytona. A race where every element—power, speed, precision, rugged durability, and luck—must come together. And now, the world's authority on endurance timepieces, Rolex, is a partner in this premier race, The Rolex 24 at Daytona.

Through each of his five 24-hour victories at the Daytona Speedway, Hurley Haywood has worn his Rolex. "When heat, dust, and vibration are the order of the day, and night," he says, "you need a tough watch.

"It's why so many of us wear Rolex."

races is night and day."

Hurley Haywood

ROLEX

Moonlighting Nissan R91 CP made hay whether or not the sun shone. Enroute to victory lane it completed 762 laps at an average speed of 112.897 mph, both new records.

ALL THROUGH THE NIGHT…
Spectator interest in the Rolex 24 at Daytona is such that the tunnel
to the speedway's infield saw a steady traffic flow even during the
wee hours.

MARTINI RACING

OFF TO A GREAT START IN '92

In January 1983, apart from a one-off appearance in Kenya's Safari Rally with Porsche some years previously, the colours of Martini Racing made their World Rally Championship debut in association with Italian manufacturer Lancia in the Monte Carlo Rally.

As if to underline the arrival of such a leading brand-name in the fast and furious world of rallysport, German driver Walter Rohrl went on to win the winter classic against all the odds at the wheel of his 2-wheel drive Martini-liveried Lancia 037 despite widespread predictions that the event would be a walkover for Audi's 4-wheel drive Quattro. By the end of the season, Martini and Lancia had notched up their first World Championship title together, the first of a total of ten Drivers' and Manufacturers' crowns to date!

In 1991, Martini Racing again triumphed in the Drivers' series thanks to Juha Kankkunen from Finland, the team also taking its fifth successive Manufacturers' title with the Lancia Delta HF Integrale 16V after a particularly nail-biting season.

And in 1992 already, Martini Racing has begun the defense of both titles in excellent fashion thanks to two outright wins with the brand new Lancia HF Integrale in Monte Carlo and in Portugal. In three events so far: Frenchman Didier Auriol dominated January's Monte to win the rally for Martini-Lancia for the second time of his career, while Kankkunen, third in Monaco, revealed some of the staggering potential of Lancia's

latest over gravel early in March to add the Rally of Portugal to a personal record which today boasts fifteen World Championship wins.

At the end of March, Kankkunen took second overall in the famous Safari Rally backed for the second successive year by Martini and today officially called the Martini Safari Rally to remain provisional leader in the Drivers' Championship, level on points with his big rival Carlos Sainz. A win for Auriol on the forthcoming Tour of Corsica in May an event he has previously won on three occasions would keep the French driver well up with Sainz and Kankkunen in the title chase, while Martini-Lancia currently enjoy a clear lead in the Manufacturers' table with a six point advantage over Toyota.

Martini colours also dominated the recent Sardinia-based European Championship qualifier, the Martini Costa Smeralda Rally, where Auriol took first place on the mixed asphalt-gravel event ahead of 28 year old teammate Andrea Aghini who, like Frenchman Philippe

Bugalski, 33, joined the team at the start of the year.

Bugalski finished his maiden event in Martini-Lancia colours, the Monte Carlo Rally, in fifth position while Aghini actually led at one stage in Portugal, his debut with the team, before retiring after an accident nine stages from home.

Following the Tour of Corsica, which ends on May 6th, the World Championship calendar visits Greece, Argentina, New Zealand, Finland, Australia, Italy, Spain, and the Ivory Coast before the final round of the season, Britain's RAC Rally, another of the sport's classics where Kankkunen made sure of his Drivers' crown with a win in 1991. Martini Racing's team management knows perfectly well that the battle is likely to be long and hard between now and the RAC Rally in November, but the collective talent of its drivers and the proven speed of the Lancia HG Integrale looks set to provide further success over the months ahead and, why not, another world title at the end of the year…

IT'S ALWAYS A GOOD YEAR.

WHEN GOOD TASTE IS MOST IMPORTANT.

Michael C. Brown

A Toyota MKIII driven by Rocky Moran, P.J. Jones, and Mark Dismore finished fourth before a record Rolex 24 at Daytona crowd. A sister car captured the pole.

Second overall, the Bud Light Jaguar took down top honors in the GTP class and the IMSA points lead. Davy Jones, David Brabham, plus IndyCar pilots Scott Pruett and Scott Goodyear shared the driving assignment.

One of the best turned out GT cars was the Martini & Rossi Camaro of Richard & Bill McDill, Tom Juckette, and Chris Schneider.

A pensive Hurley Haywood, the winningest Rolex 24 at Daytona driver, ponders the brake problem on his 0123 Porsche that cooled his chances of earning a sixth victory in the classic.

BIG LEAD…
Whistler Mustang built up a margin sufficient enough to allow parking the car before the end and still come out on top in the GTS category.

Steve Swope

EIGHT IN A ROW...
Jack Roush and Ford Motor Company racked up their 8th consecutive victory in the big GT class. Roush accepts the trophy presented by Rolex Watch U.S.A. President Roland Puton. Mark Martin, Wally Dallenbach Jr., Robby Gordon, and Dorsey Schroeder shared the driving duties in the Whistler Mustang.

RECORD SPEED, RECORD DISTANCE...
Massahiro Hasemi, Kazuyoshi Hoshino, Toshio Suzuki, and Anders Olofsson set new marks for the 24 Hours in their Nissan R91 CP "LeMans" type car. Rolex Watch U.S.A. President Roland Puton presented them with handsome timepieces, Rolex, naturally.

ROLEX 24 AT DAYTONA
February 1, 1992
OFFICIAL RESULTS

FIN POS	CLS POS	STR POS	CAR NO.	DRIVERS	ENTRANT	CAR	LAPS	STATUS
1	1X	2	23X	MASSAHIRO HASEMI / KAZUYOSHI HOSHINO / TOSHIO SUZUKI / ANDERS OLOFSSON	Nissan Mtrsprt Int'l	Nissan R91 CP	762	Running
2	1	7	2	DAVY JONES / DAVID BRABHAM / SCOTT PRUETT / SCOTT GOODYEAR	Bud Light / Jaguar RCG	Jaguar XJR-12 D	753	Running
3	2	9	52	HURLEY HAYWOOD / EJE ELGH / ROLAND RATZENBERGER / SCOTT BRAYTON	Team 0123	Porsche 962	749	Running
4	3	6	98	ROCKY MORAN / P J JONES / MARK DISMORE	All American Racers	Toyota Egl. MKIII	739	Running
5	1L	14	49L	PARKER JOHNSTONE / DAN MARVIN / JIM VASSER / STEVE CAMERON	Acura	Acura Spice	681	Running
6	2L	17	44L	ANDY EVANS / FERMIN VELEZ / LON BENDER / DOMINIC DOBSON	Scandia Eng	Buick Kudzu	654	Running
7	1*	37	82*	DICK GREER / AL BACON / PETER URIA / MIKE MEES	Wendy's Race Team	Mazda RX-7	636	Running
8	2X	5	27X	VOLKER WEIDLER / MAURO MARTINI / JEFF KROSNOFF	Nova Eng	Nissan R91 CP	635	Running
9	1#	19	15#	WALLY DALLENBACH / DORSEY SCHROEDER / ROBBY GORDON	Whistler Mustang	Ford Mustang	614 NR	Engine
10	2#	20	51#	DARIN BRASSFIELD / GEORGE ROBINSON / JEFF KLINE / PAUL GENTILOZZI	Olivetti Oldsmobile	Oldsmobile Cutlass	590	Running
11	4	1	99	JUAN FANGIO, II / ANDY WALLACE / KENNY ACHESON	All American Racers	Toyota Eagle MKIII	584	Running
12	2*	35	24*	EDUARDO DIBOS / JUAN DIBOS / RAUL ORLANDINI	Alberti Mtrsprts	Mazda MX-6	573	Running
13	3*	31	95*	BOB LEITZINGER / DAVID LORING / CHUCK KURTZ / BUTCH LEITZINGER	Fastcolor Auto Art	Nissan 240SX	566	Running
14	3#	21	11#	JIM STEVENS / CALVIN FISH / MARK MARTIN / ROBBIE BUHL	Whistler Mustang	Ford Mustang	539	Running
15	4*	28	96*	DAVID LORING / CHUCK KURTZ / DAN ROBSON / DON KNOWLES	Fastcolor Auto Art	Nissan 240SX	538	Running
16	4#	15	75#	JEREMY DALE / JOHNNY O'CONNELL / JOHN MORTON	Nissan	Nissan 300ZX	531	Running
17	5#	36	50#	OMA KIMBROUGH / MARK MONTGOMERY / ROBERT McELHENY / GARY SWANANDER / JON LEWIS / RAAN RODRIGUEZ / HOYT OVERBAGH	Slick 50	Chevrolet Camaro	529	Running
18	5*	39	26*	JOE PEZZA / JACK REFENNING / ALEX PADILLA / JOHN SHELDON	Border Cantina	Porsche 911	506	Running
19	5	3	30	HANS STUCK / FRANK JELINSKI / GIANPIERO MORETTI / HENRI PESCAROLO	Momo	Porsche 962C	503 NR	Electrical
20	6*	34	0*	JOHN FERGUS / BOBBY AKIN JR / NEIL HANNEMANN	Infinity / Dodge / Ftr	Dodge Daytona	471	Running
21	7*	32	37*	ROB WILSON / LUCIO BERNAL / FELIPE SOLANO / MIGUEL MOREJON	Botero Rcg Team	Mazda MX-6	465 NR	Mechanical
22	6#	44	21#	KENT PAINTER / ROBERT BORDERS / JOHN ANNIS / ROBERT KAHN / JOHN MACALUSO	Western Chemical	Chevrolet Camaro	465	Running
23	8*	47	72*	JAY KJOLLER / STEVE VOLK / ROBIN BOONE	Renntech Per System	Porsche 911	432	Running
24	3L	24	36L	HOWARD KATZ / JOHN GROOMS / FRANK JELLINEK / JIM DOWNING	Downing / Atlanta	Mazda Kudzu	426 NR	Mechanical
25	7#	48	67#	PAUL MAZZACANE / HENRY BROSNAHAM / STEVE BURGNER / BOBBY SCOLO	Mazkar Racing	Chevrolet Camaro	389	Running
26	3X	8	13X	BOB WOLLEK / PASCAL FABRE / LIONEL ROBERT	Radio Nostalgie	Porsche Courage	387 NR	Accident
27	4L	33	33L	ULI BIERI / VITO SCAVONE / HEINZ WIRTH / ANDREW HEPWORTH	Molson Take Care	Ferrari Tiga	349 NR	Engine
28	9*	45	57*	FRANK DEL VECCHIO / JOE DANAHER / BILL SARGIS / MARK KENT / REED KRYDER	Kryderacing	Nissan 240SX	345	Running
29	6	4	7	JOHN WINTER / MASSIMO SIGALA / OSCAR LARRAURI / BERND SCHNEIDER	Torno	Porsche 962C	327 NR	Engine
30	10*	46	58*	SAM SHALALA / ANDRE TOENNIS / TIM McADAM / CHARLES MONK / DAN PASTORINI	Pro-Technik	Porsche 911	313	Running
31	8#	22	41#	IRV HOERR / JACK BALDWIN	Olivetti Oldsmobile	Oldsmobile Cutlass	312 NR	Mechanical
32	9#	29	25#	DALE KREIDER / BILL ADAMS / JOHN DUKE / JOHN GOODING	OMI Oil Treatment	Oldsmobile Cutlass	289 NR	Engine
33	5L	25	6L	MEL BUTT / RON ZITZA / TOMMY JOHNSON / ROB ROBERTSON	MAB Rcg	Buick Tiga	279 NR	Engine
34	7	12	83	GEOFF BRABHAM / CHIP ROBINSON / BOB EARL / ARIE LUYENDYK	Nissan Perf Tech	Nissan R90 C	272 NR	Engine
35	8	10	12	FRANCOIS MIGAULT / TOMAS LOPEZ / DAVID TENNYSON	Radio Nostalgie	Porsche Courage	220 NR	Engine
36	11*	43	05*	HENRY CAMFERDAM / PHIL KRUEGER / GARY DRUMMOND	Support Net Rcg	Mazda MX-6	214 NR	Mechanical
37	9	11	4	WAYNE TAYLOR / JEFF PURNER / HUGH FULLER / HIDESHI MATZUDA	Applebee's Inter	Chevrolet Spice	213 NR	Engine
38	10#	26	35#	RICHARD McDILL / BILL McDILL / TOM JUCKETTE / CHRIS SCHNEIDER	Martini & Rossi	Chevrolet Camaro	204	Running
39	12*	42	69*	BRAD HOYT / ANDY PILGRIM / JOHN PETRICK	North Coast Rcg	Mazda RX-7	195 NR	Engine
40	6L	16	48L	COSTAS LOS / BOB LESNETT / KAZUO SHIMIZU / RUGGERO MELGRATI	Acura	Acura Spice	168 NR	Gearbox
41	10	13	84	DEREK DALY / STEVE MILLEN / GARY BRABHAM	Nissan Perf Tech	Nissan R90 C	150 NR	Accident
42	11#	18	76#	JOHNNY O'CONNELL / JOHN MORTON	Nissan	Nissan 300ZX	144 NR	Electrical
43	7L	23	9L	CHARLES MORGAN / JIM PACE / KEN KNOTT	Essex Rcg Service	Buick Kudzu	129 NR	Accident
44	8L	27	17L	CARLOS BOBEDA / KEN PARSCHAUER	Carlos Bobeda Rcg	Buick Spice	125 NR	Accident
45	13*	41	73*	JACK LEWIS / TAYLOR ROBERTSON / BILL FERRAN	Jack Lewis Ent Ltd	Porsche 911	115 NR	Accident
46	14*	40	55*	BOB SCHADER / PHIL MAHRE	GTE / Mobilnet	Mazda MX-6	94 NR	Accident
47	15*	38	71*	AMOS JOHNSON / SCOTT HOERR	Oldsmobile Mtrsprts	Oldsmobile Achieva	89 NR	Engine
48	9L	49	40L	JOHNNY UNSER	Molson Take Care	Ford Alba	47 NR	Mechanical
49	12#	30	22#	LUIS SEREIX	J&B Mtrsprts	Chevrolet Camaro	32 NR	Engine

TIME OF RACE: 24:01:41.598   **L** = Camel Lights   **+ # =** GT Supreme   *** =** GTU   **X** = Non-Standard Class
WINNING SPEED: 112.897 mph for 762 laps (2,712.720 miles) REC   **NR** = Not running at finish
MARGIN OF VICTORY: 9 laps, 51.063 seconds   **REC** = New record

FASTEST LAPS: GTP: Juan Fangio, II, lap 7, 126.962 mph REC
LeMans Cars: Massahiro Hasemi, lap 5, 130.118 mph REC
Camel Lights: Parker Johnstone, lap 24, 115.450 mph REC
GT Supreme: John Morton, lap 6, 114.292 mph
GTU: David Loring, lap 29, 103.209 mph

After their triumphant appearance in Victory Circle, the winning Japanese team had a private celebration. Martini & Rossi Asti Spumante supplied the bubbles.

Rick Bannerot

Dan Gurney drove this Lotus 19 to victory in the 1962 Daytona Continental.

ROLEX LEGENDS AT DAYTONA

Thirty six sports racing cars of distinction, including five previous winners of the Daytona 24 Hours, all Porsches, took the flag for the '92 Rolex Legends at Daytona. Unquestioned star of the multi-million dollar collection was the 1961 Lotus 19 driven by Dan Gurney to the checkered flag in the 1962 Daytona Continental, forerunner of the 24 Hours and the first FIA sanctioned event at Daytona. The winning Porsches, three 935s and two 962s, tied for unofficial runner-up honors in crowd acclaim.

A quartet of Porsche 935s, including the 1983 Daytona 24 Hour winner (no. 6) driven by Bob Wollek, Claude Ballot-Lena, Preston Henn, and A.J. Foyt. Porsche has won more Rolex 24s at Daytona than any other make, has never finished lower than third.

Ice water in their veins. Prestone in their engines.

Nine out of ten NASCAR racing teams use Prestone.® We make it better than we have to. FIRST BRANDS

DAYTONA 500 BY STP QUALIFYING

FORD-POWERED TEAMMATES STERLING MARLIN AND BILL ELLIOTT NAIL DOWN FRONT ROW STARTING POSITIONS

By Tom Higgins

As generally predicted by garage area insiders, Ford drivers Sterling Marlin and Bill Elliott swept the Daytona 500 front row starting positions for team owner Junior Johnson.

Marlin took the Busch pole with a lap of 192.213 mph, flashing around the 2.5-mile track in 46.823 seconds. Predictably it was the slowest time trial session for the season-opening NASCAR Winston Cup Series classic since Cale Yarborough's speed of 187.536 was fastest in 1978. NASCAR's carburetor restrictor plate regulations performed as designed, "slow 'em down a bit but not enough to take away the excitement".

Elliott, joining Johnson's operation based in Wilkes County, NC, this season as a nominal teammate to Marlin and set to make his first official start for the operation in the "500" next Sunday, made a stout run at Marlin's clocking. He missed by a mere three-hundredths of a second. Elliott's speed was 192.090, his time 46.853 seconds, good enough for the second front row starting position.

Only the Johnson-fielded duo topped 192 mph and that made them just the second set of teammates to start 1-2 in stock car racing's biggest, richest event dating to 1959. Chevrolet drivers Ken Schrader and Darrell Waltrip did it in 1989 when both drove for Rick Hendrick.

"This is a big thrill, I'm really pleased," said a grinning Marlin after taking his third straight pole position for races in which a carburetor restrictor plate is required to reduce speed for safety. He also was fastest for the Pepsi 400 at Daytona last July and the DieHard 500 at Talladega (Ala.) Superspeedway later that month.

"I came down here with my daddy (retired driver Clifton "Coo Coo" Marlin) in the late 1960s when I was seven or eight and I've been in awe of this speedway ever since," continued the younger Marlin after his big splash in the qualifying session, during which only the first two starting spots for the 500 were locked in. Two later 125-mile races and additional time trials determine the rest of the lineup.

"Running this good for the Daytona 500 is awful special, and I've got to thank my crew chief, Mike Beam, the rest of the boys on the team and engine builder J.V. Reins for it," said Marlin. "We tested so much here in December and January that I thought we were going to take up permanent residence. This is the same engine we've used for all three of those poles. Other engines showed up just as good on the dyno, but once in the car this one works way the best."

"Now we need to win a race, and I believe we're ready to do that. I feel we'll win maybe four this year."

Marlin, 34, is 0-for-219 in Winston Cup starts dating to 1976. He has come close often and lists five runnerup finishes, including second place to Ernie Irvan in the Daytona 500 a year ago. Marlin said he "worried" when the wind rose and started blowing down the long backstretch just before qualifying began. "We thought about re-gearing the car on account of it, but didn't," he said. "The wind cost me about 150 rpms. It had the same effect a headwind does on a small airplane."

The wind was blowing at 10.3 mph when Marlin qualified. It appeared to intensify, and Elliott's crew did change to a lower gear to adjust for that, but it wasn't enough. "It was so close on the clock, anything could have turned it around the other way," said Elliott. "Sterling and his team put a hurting on us, but we're competitive and I feel rejuvenated."

Marlin traced the surprisingly slow pace to that headwind and a rear deck spoiler increased to 240 square inches by NASCAR as a further safety move. "The bigger spoiler increases aerodynamic drag and that slows you some," said the pole winner.

Some observers suggested that Marlin might have included noticeably tighter inspections of the cars by the NASCAR officials headed by new technical director Gary Nelson.

Asked what Johnson had to say of the sweep, Marlin smiled and replied, "I don't know. He got on an airplane and headed to Wilkes County before time trials were over. Junior isn't too excitable. He'd probably just have smiled and told us we did a good job." Mark Martin and a surprising Dorsey Schroeder, the former road racing champion, were third and fourth fastest in Fords. Schroeder qualified with a borrowed engine after three of his Junie Donlavey team's motors failed in practice.

Fastest in a General Motors car was Harry Gant, fifth at 190.702 in an Olds. Completing the top

10: Phil Parsons, Ford; Davey Allison, Ford; Winston Cup champion Dale Earnhardt, Chevrolet; Brett Bodine, Ford; and Richard Petty, Pontiac.

"At least we had the fastest Chevy," said Earnhardt still seeking his first Daytona 500 win, "I think we'll be alright for the '125s' and the '500', 'cause we've got a good-handling car and that's what it'll take."

Petty is qualifying for his last Daytona 500 before retiring as a driver at the end of the season. He has won the race a record seven times. Said Petty: "Pretty good, although we figured to be a little faster. We're satisfied. I

think we can run pretty well with the car in race trim."

Among the drivers surprisingly far back in opening round time trials: Geoff Bodine, winner of the Busch Clash 24 hours earlier, 15th in a Ford; Ernie Irvan, Chevy, 18th; 1989 Daytona 500 winner and three-time Winston Cup champion Darrell Waltrip, Chevy, 21st; Alan Kulwicki, Ford, 29th; Ken Schrader, winner of Daytona 500 poles 1988 through '90, Chevy, 31st; 1989 national champion Rusty Wallace, Pontiac, 34th; and '90 Daytona 500 victor Derrike Cope, Chevy, 35th.

GATORADE 125-MILE QUALIFYING RACES

EARNHARDT AND ELLIOTT THE WINNERS IN "500" PREVIEW

By Tom Higgins

Dale Earnhardt and Bill Elliott drove to victories in drastically different Gatorade 125-mile qualifying races leading to the Daytona 500.

There was nothing "twin-like" about the Daytona International Speedway preliminaries before a crowd estimated at 100,000.

Earnhardt charged to the checkered flag in a Chevrolet just feet ahead of Ford foe Mark Martin in a wreck-marred opener. Richard Petty, starting the final season of his storied career, was just one of the victims.

Petty, who counts seven Daytona 500 by STP wins among his record 200 triumphs, was forced into a backup car for the "500" — as were several other drivers — because of the accidents. Petty will line up 32nd to begin the classic for the final time.

Elliott's Ford flashed to the line first in the second race that produced only one minor spin.

The races determined starting positions 3-30 in the "500", stock car racing's most important event. Sterling Marlin, an accident casualty in the first 50-lapper at the 2.5-mile track, and nominal teammate Elliott took the front row spots last Sunday in time trials with laps slightly over 192 mph.

Positions 31-42 are set by qualifying speeds and provisional starting opportunities.

Martin made a strong "slingshot," aerodynamic passing move of Earnhardt off Turn 4 on the final lap of the first 125-mile race. However, Chevy-driving Ernie Irvan nosed behind Earnhardt and gave the Winston Cup champion the draft-generated impetus to surge to the stripe three-fourths of a car length ahead. Defending "500" champion Irvan was third, followed by Greg Sacks in a Chevy and Harry Gant in an Olds.

"I think Mark would have gotten me if Ernie hadn't been there," Earnhardt, who led 23 laps, including the final 10, said after a third straight 125 win and fifth overall. "I felt I had to get by Mark (on a restart on Lap 41 following a crash involving Dale Jarrett and Kyle Petty) to have a shot at winning. I wanted to be in front and try to command. I was lucky to be able to do that.

"On the last lap there was a slow car I drafted for some help, still Mark was strong enough to come up outside of me. I knew he was there. I could feel the air. He pulled a little ahead. Luckily, Ernie followed me and I got back in front. Winning a "125" gets you pumped up for Sunday."

Said Martin, who led Laps 20-40: "I dropped back a bit the last lap and managed a good run that got me beside Dale on the outside, but I couldn't buck the wind. Dale and Ernie did a great job. We took our best shot at 'em, but didn't have a drafting partner to help us out. I'd like to have won, but we've got something we can go racing with for 500 miles on Sunday."

Observed Irvan: "You can't cut off the hand that feeds you. Dale and I both are in Chevrolets. It was a choice I had to make. He owes me one."

The worst of the opener's three wrecks occurred on Lap 5 and generally was traced to the instability of the cars in traffic because of the aerodynamic slipstream. There appeared to be contact between the Fords of Martin and Alan Kulwicki, with the latter slipping sideways off Turn 4. Swept into the accident was the Pontiac of Richard Petty, plus Terry Labonte, Chevy; A.J. Foyt, Olds; Rick Wilson, Ford; Hut Stricklin, Chevy; Dave Mader III, Chevy; and Ben Hess, Ford.

Kulwicki, Labonte, Foyt, Wilson and Stricklin, like Richard Petty, were forced to backups. Mader and Hess didn't make the race.

"I can't say exactly what happened, it felt like I got bumped," said Kulwicki who emerged limping. "Then I got hit really hard on both sides."

Said Richard Petty: "The No. 7 car (Kulwicki) came out of the line sideways, then everybody went everywhere. We'll try again Sunday."

Marlin spun off Turn 4 on Lap 20 in an incident which also appeared to be triggered by tricky aerodynamics when

Earnhardt drove up close behind the Ford. "There was no warning or nothing, then boom," said Marlin. "That's the quickest a car ever has got out from under me. Everytime I spun I saw the wall and hoped to stay out of it." Marlin did, saving his car for Sunday.

"When Sterling broke loose he got out of the gas and I got on the brakes, but I still tapped him," said Earnhardt. "It wasn't anyone's fault. I hate that he spun and I hope he's not too awful mad."

Jarrett, who had run strongly in Joe Gibbs' Chevy, lost control on Lap 36 in Turn 4 and swept Kyle Petty's Pontiac into the trouble with him. Both had to turn to backup cars. "I just messed up," Jarrett said manfully. "I'm sorry Kyle got in it. The car broke loose when the draft was taken off the spoiler."

Elliott led all the second race but the 41st lap in a Junior Johnson team Ford.   Davey Allison, forced into a backup Thunderbird by an accident Wednesday, charged from the rear of the field to the front very quickly.

Elliott won by 1½ car lengths over the surprisingly strong T-bird of Morgan Shepherd, with Allison a close third. Ricky Rudd took fourth in a Chevy, and Pontiac's Michael Waltrip outdueled his older brother Darrell in a Chevy for fifth. "I think the second race was incident free 'cause everybody saw what happened in the first race," said Elliott. "They said, 'Well, if the car will drive, we'll run it and if it ain't driving, we'll take what we can get and save it for the 500.'"

Linda McQueeney

FIRST GATORADE TWIN 125 MILE QUALIFYING RACE
February 13, 1992
OFFICIAL RESULTS

FIN POS	STR POS	CAR NO.	DRIVER	TEAM/CAR	LAPS	MONEY	STATUS
1	4	3	DALE EARNHARDT	GM Goodwrench Chevrolet	50	$35,400	Running
2	2	6	MARK MARTIN	Valvoline Ford	50	22,200	Running
3	9	4	ERNIE IRVAN	Kodak Film Chevrolet	50	15,200	Running
4	12	41	GREG SACKS	Kellogg's Chevrolet	50	10,200	Running
5	19	33	HARRY GANT	Skoal Bandit Oldsmobile	50	8,200	Running
6	15	1	RICK MAST	Skoal Classic Oldsmobile	50	5,100	Running
7	21	25	KEN SCHRADER	Kodiak Chevrolet	50	4,800	Running
8	16	2	RUSTY WALLACE	Miller Genuine Draft Pontiac	50	4,650	Running
9	3	9	PHIL PARSONS	Melling Racing Ford	50	4,500	Running
10	27	03	KERRY TEAGUE*	Team USA Oldsmobile	50	4,250	Running
11	17	71	DAVE MARCIS	Big Apple Market Chevrolet	50	4,100	Running
12	24	73	PHIL BARKDOLL	X1R Oldsmobile	50	3,950	Running
13	29	0	DELMA COWART	Master's Economy Inn Ford	50	3,800	Running
14	23	77	MIKE POTTER	Kenova Construction Chevrolet	50	3,650	Running
15	22	99	BRAD TEAGUE	Traffic Engineering Chevrolet	49	3,500	Running
16	28	59	ANDY BELMONT*	Slick 50 Ford	49	3,250	Running
17	13	12	HUT STRICKLIN	Raybestos Chevrolet	46	3,100	Running
18	8	18	DALE JARRETT	Interstate Batteries Chevrolet	35	2,950	Accident
19	6	42	KYLE PETTY	Mello Yello Pontiac	35	2,800	Accident
20	25	23	EDDIE BIERSCHWALE	SpitFire Oldsmobile	33	2,700	Running
21	10	16	WALLY DALLENBACH	Keystone Ford	21	2,500	Eng. Fail.
22	1	22	STERLING MARLIN	Maxwell House Coffee Ford	19	2,900	Accident
23	5	43	RICHARD PETTY	STP Pontiac	8	2,300	Accident
24	14	7	ALAN KULWICKI	Hooters Ford	4	2,200	Accident
25	7	94	TERRY LABONTE	Sunoco Chevrolet	4	2,100	Accident
26	20	14	A.J. FOYT	Copenhagen Oldsmobile	4	2,000	Accident
27	11	8	RICK WILSON	SNICKERS Ford	4	1,900	Accident
28	18	13	DAVE MADER III	Seal-Tech Mtrsprts Chevrolet	4	1,850	Accident
29	26	62	BEN HESS	Gray Racing Ford	4	1,750	Accident

TIME OF RACE: 01:04:25
AVERAGE SPEED: 116.430 mph
MARGIN OF VICTORY: ¾ car length

CAUTION FLAGS: 3 flags for 20 laps
LEAD CHANGES: 4 lead changes, 3 drivers
*NASCAR Winston Cup Rookie of the Year Candidate

Blushing Bill Elliott is double teamed by the Unocal girls after winning the Gatorade Twin 125 qualifying race no. 2.

Pontiac pace car got a good workout in the first Gatorade Twin 125 qualifying race in which three crashes took out ten cars.

SECOND GATORADE TWIN 125 MILE QUALIFYING RACE
February 13, 1992
OFFICIAL RESULTS

FIN POS	STR POS	CAR NO.	DRIVER	TEAM/CAR	LAPS	MONEY	STATUS
1	1	11	BILL ELLIOTT	Budweiser Ford	50	$35,200	Running
2	19	21	MORGAN SHEPHERD	Citgo Ford	50	22,200	Running
3	3	28	DAVEY ALLISON	Havoline Ford	50	15,200	Running
4	5	5	RICKY RUDD	Tide Chevrolet	50	10,200	Running
5	8	30	MICHAEL WALTRIP	Pennzoil Pontiac	50	8,200	Running
6	10	17	DARRELL WALTRIP	Western Auto Chevrolet	50	5,100	Running
7	6	66	CHAD LITTLE	TropArtic Ford	50	4,800	Running
8	7	15	GEOFF BODINE	Motorcraft Ford	50	4,650	Running
9	4	26	BRETT BODINE	Quaker State Ford	50	4,500	Running
10	16	10	DERRIKE COPE	Purolator Chevrolet	50	4,250	Running
11	14	68	BOBBY HAMILTON	Country Time Oldsmobile	50	4,100	Running
12	21	47	BUDDY BAKER	Close Racing Oldsmobile	50	3,950	Running
13	24	31	BOBBY HILLIN, JR.	Team Ireland Chevrolet	50	3,800	Running
14	11	75	DICK TRICKLE	Rahmoc Oldsmobile	50	3,650	Running
15	13	49	STANLEY SMITH	Ameritron Batteries Chevrolet	50	3,500	Running
16	2	90	DORSEY SCHROEDER	Whistler Radar Ford	50	3,750	Running
17	20	83	LAKE SPEED	Lurex Chevrolet	49	3,100	Running
18	15	89	JIM SAUTER	Evinrude Pontiac	49	2,950	Running
19	17	20	MIKE WALLACE	Daily's 1st Ade Oldsmobile	49	2,800	Running
20	12	55	TED MUSGRAVE	Jasper Engines Chevrolet	49	2,700	Running
21	25	98	JIMMY SPENCER	Moly Black Gold Chevrolet	49	2,500	Running
22	26	13	MIKE SKINNER	Glidden Paints Chevrolet	49	2,400	Running
23	27	88	JOE BOOHER	88 Racing Pontiac	49	2,300	Running
24	18	50	CLAY YOUNG*	AFLAC Pontiac	49	2,200	Running
25	28	48	JAMES HYLTON	Rumple Furniture Chevrolet	49	2,100	Running
26	23	52	JIMMY MEANS	Means Racing Pontiac	49	2,000	Running
27	22	97	MARK GIBSON	Collins Racing Oldsmobile	46	1,900	Running
28	9	95	BOB SCHACHT*	Shoneys Oldsmobile	7	1,850	Eng. Fail.

TIME OF RACE: 00:44:10
AVERAGE SPEED: 169.811 mph
MARGIN OF VICTORY: 1½ car length

CAUTION FLAGS: 1 flag for 4 laps
LEAD CHANGES: 2 lead changes, 2 drivers
*NASCAR Winston Cup Rookie of the Year Candidate

Steve Swope

Dan Bianchi

Starting 1st
STERLING MARLIN, Car No. 22
Maxwell House Coffee Ford, Speed 192.213

Starting 2nd
BILL ELLIOTT, Car No. 11
Budweiser Ford, Speed 192.090

Steve Swope

Starting 3rd
DALE EARNHARDT, Car No. 3
GM Goodwrench Chevrolet, 1st, Qualifying Race No. 1

Starting 4th
MORGAN SHEPHERD, Car No. 21
Citgo Ford, 2nd, Qualifying Race No. 2

Dan Bianchi

Starting 5th
MARK MARTIN, Car No. 6
Valvoline Ford, 2nd, Qualifying Race No. 1

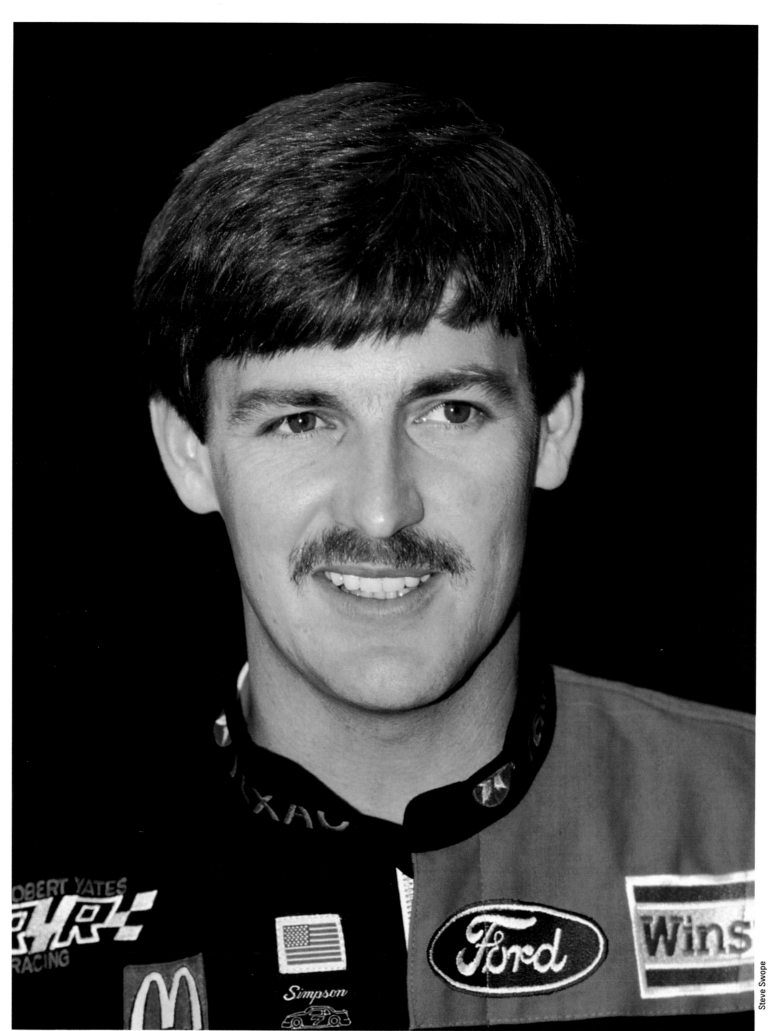

Steve Swope

Starting 6th
DAVEY ALLISON, Car No. 28
Havoline Ford, 3rd, Qualifying Race No. 2

44

Starting 7th
ERNIE IRVAN, Car No. 4
Kodak Film Chevrolet, 3rd, Qualifying Race No. 1

Dan Bianchi

Starting 8th
RICKY RUDD, Car No. 5
Tide Chevrolet, 4th, Qualifying Race No. 2

Starting 9th
GREG SACKS, Car No. 41
Kellogg's Chevrolet, 4th, Qualifying Race No. 1

Linda McQueeney

Starting 10th
MICHAEL WALTRIP, Car No. 30
Pennzoil Pontiac, 5th, Qualifying Race No. 2

Starting 11th
HARRY GANT, Car No. 33
Skoal Bandit Oldsmobile, 5th, Qualifying Race No. 1

Linda McQueeney

Starting 12th
DARRELL WALTRIP, Car No. 17
Western Auto Chevrolet, 6th, Qualifying Race No. 2

Dan Bianchi

Starting 13th
RICK MAST, Car No. 1
Skoal Classic Oldsmobile, 6th, Qualifying Race No. 1

Starting 14th
CHAD LITTLE, Car No. 66
TropArtic Ford, 7th, Qualifying Race No. 2

Starting 15th
KEN SCHRADER, Car No. 25
Kodiak Chevrolet, 7th, Qualifying Race No. 1

Starting 16th
GEOFF BODINE, Car No. 15
Motorcraft Ford, 8th, Qualifying Race No. 2

Dan Bianchi

Starting 17th
RUSTY WALLACE, Car No. 2
Miller Genuine Draft Pontiac, 8th, Qualifying Race No. 1

Starting 18th
BRETT BODINE, Car No. 26
Quaker State Ford, 9th, Qualifying Race No. 2

Steve Swope

56

Dan Bianchi

Starting 19th
PHIL PARSONS, Car No. 9
Melling Racing Ford, 9th, Qualifying Race No. 1

Starting 20th
DERRIKE COPE, Car No. 10
Purolator Chevrolet, 10th, Qualifying Race No. 2

Starting 21st
KERRY TEAGUE, Car No. 03*
Team USA Oldsmobile, 10th, Qualifying Race No. 1

Starting 22nd
BOBBY HAMILTON, Car No. 68
Country Time Oldsmobile, 11th, Qualifying Race No. 2

Starting 23rd
DAVE MARCIS, Car No. 71
Big Apple Market Chevrolet, 11th, Qualifying Race No. 1

Dan Bianchi

Ron McQueeney

Starting 24th
BUDDY BAKER, Car No. 47
Close Racing Oldsmobile, 12th, Qualifying Race No. 2

Dan Bianchi

Starting 25th
PHIL BARKDOLL, Car No. 73
X1R Oldsmobile, 12th, Qualifying Race No. 1

Starting 26th
BOBBY HILLIN JR., Car No. 31
Team Ireland Chevrolet, 13th, Qualifying Race No. 2

Dan Bianchi

Starting 27th
DELMA COWART, Car No. 0
Master's Economy Inn Ford, 13th, Qualifying Race No. 1

Dan Bianchi

Linda McQueeney

Starting 28th
DICK TRICKLE, Car No. 75
Rahmoc Oldsmobile, 14th, Qualifying Race No. 2

62

Starting 29th
MIKE POTTER, Car No. 77
Kenova Construction Chevrolet, 14th, Qualifying Race No. 1

Dan Bianchi

Dan Bianchi

Starting 30th
STANLEY SMITH, Car No. 49
Ameritron Batteries Chevrolet, 15th, Qualifying Race No. 2

Starting 31st
DORSEY SCHROEDER, Car No. 90
Whistler Radar Ford, Speed 191.404

Linda McQueeney

63

Starting 32nd
RICHARD PETTY, Car No. 43
STP Pontiac, Speed 189.909

Starting 33rd
KYLE PETTY, Car No. 42
Mello Yello Pontiac, Speed 189.717

Dan Bianchi

Starting 34th
TERRY LABONTE, Car No. 94
Sunoco Chevrolet, Speed 188.897

Steve Swope

Starting 35th
DALE JARRETT, Car No. 18
Interstate Batteries Chevrolet, Speed 188.644

Starting 36th
BOB SCHACHT, Car No. 95*
Shoneys Oldsmobile, Speed 188.225

Dan Bianchi

67

Starting 37th
WALLY DALLENBACH JR., Car No. 16
Keystone Ford, Speed 188.206

Dan Bianchi

Linda McQueeney

Starting 38th
RICK WILSON, Car No. 8
SNICKERS Ford, Speed 187.993

Starting 41st
ALAN KULWICKI, Car No. 7
Hooters Ford, Provisional Starting Position

Linda McQueeney

Starting 39th
A. J. FOYT, Car No. 14
Copenhagen Oldsmobile, Speed 187.903

Linda McQueeney

Dan Bianchi

Starting 40th
TED MUSGRAVE, Car No. 55
Jasper Engines Chevrolet, Speed 187.336

Starting 42nd
HUT STRICKLIN, Car No. 12
Raybestos Chevrolet, Provisional Starting Position

Dan Bianchi

Starting positions 1 and 2 based on speed attained on the first day of official qualifications, positions 3 through 30 on results of the Twin 125 Mile Qualifying races. Positions 31 through 40 based on qualifying speeds. Two provisional starting positions based on 1992 Winston Cup Car Owner Point Standings. Users of back-up cars moved to back of the field.
* NASCAR Winston Cup Rookie of the Year Candidate

Mark Martin won the last race of the '91 season, notched five Busch poles during the campaign, went into the '92 500 as one of the favorites. Here he strolls pit lane hand in hand with wife Arlene.

Dan Bianchi

Ricky and Linda Rudd go over their laundry list while waiting for the Tide Chevrolet to be wheeled out.

Linda McQueeney

Car owner Felix Sabates and Kyle Petty review strategy prior to the 500.

Steve Swope

Michael Waltrip bench races Sterling Marlin prior to the countdown for the 500.

Linda McQueeney

1989 Winston Cup champion Rusty Wallace, right, offers a few helpful hints to first time Daytona 500 by STP starter Dorsey Schroeder.

Gary Nelson, NASCAR's new technical director, quickly earned the respect of the racing fraternity.

Linda McQueeney

THE LOOK OF A WINNER...
Davey Allison's sharp eyes and reflexes steered him clear of the crash that down-graded the leaders on lap 92, swept him into victory circle.

DAYTONA 500 BY STP

14 CAR CRASH TAKES OUT THE LEADERS, DAVEY ALLISON AVOIDS IT, TAKES DOWN WINNER'S $224,000

By Tom Higgins

Davey Allison made a heady move to avoid a wrecking trio of leaders just feet ahead of him and dominated the Daytona 500 by STP afterward to win the NASCAR Winston Cup Series' biggest stock car race for the first time.

As Ford-powered teammates Sterling Marlin and Bill Elliott bumped, along with Chevrolet driver Ernie Irvan, and then spun out of control on the backstretch at Daytona International Speedway, Allison whipped his Thunderbird to the outside and cleared the trouble that swept up 12 other cars, including several top contenders.

Incredibly, the chain reaction crash on the 92nd of 200 laps at the 2.5-mile track resulted in only one slight injury, Ken Schrader's sprained ankle.

But it outright eliminated the cars of Dale Jarrett, Chad Little, Schrader and pole winner Marlin, while erasing the victory chances of Dale Earnhardt, Mark Martin, Darrell Waltrip, Elliott, Hut Stricklin and Richard Petty, the seven-time winner of the 500, who was making his last start in the race.

After the accident Allison, driving the Charlotte-based Robert Yates Racing team's No. 28 Ford, led all 98 of the remaining green flag laps. He was in front 127 laps overall in the backup machine substituted after an accident in practice damaged the primary T-bird last Wednesday.

"I saw that thing, the wreck, getting ready to happen," said Allison, who was in fourth spot as Elliott and Irvan attempted to maneuver around either side of leader Marlin coming off Turn 2. "I slowed so I'd have a chance to miss it and I got by clean."

Allison's famous father, Bobby, won the 500 three times. When Bobby, now a team owner, last triumphed in 1988, Davey finished second in a heart warming family tussle.

In joining Petty, previously the only second generation driver to capture the classic, the younger Allison finished two car-lengths ahead of runnerup Morgan Shepherd, making his first start in the Wood Brothers Ford.

Geoff Bodine and Alan Kulwicki, the latter rallying from 41st starting position, gave Thunderbirds a sweep of the top four positions. Dick Trickle finished fifth, the only other driver on the lead lap, in the RahMoc team's unsponsored Olds.

Completing the top 10: Kyle Petty, Pontiac; Terry Labonte, Chevy; Ted Musgrave, Chevy; Winston Cup champion Earnhardt, Chevy; and Phil Parsons, Ford. It's the best-ever finish for Musgrave, a rookie in 1991.

"Morgan is a tough ol' veteran," Allison, 30, said of his closest pursuer after his 14th victory, including three of the last four races dating to autumn of '91 in cars prepared by a Larry McReynolds-led crew. "I finished

second to that Wood Brothers car (with Jarrett then driving it) last August at Michigan. I was praying to God those last laps to let me make the right moves." His prayers were answered.

The victory was worth $244,040 to the Yates team, second largest regular season purse in NASCAR history. To collect it, Allison averaged 160.256 mph despite four caution flags for 22 laps.

Allison and Shepherd were left to decide the outcome between themselves when the potent Pontiac of Michael Waltrip burned a piston as he ran second just eight laps from the finish. "We were in a position to at least try to make a run for the win," said Waltrip. "The Daytona 500 can be cruel. I think we could have made it interesting."

"I would have to have had some help (an aerodynamic drafting partner) for a shot at Davey," said Shepherd after his best Daytona 500 finish. "He was a little stronger than us. If Michael could have stayed in, there's no telling what would have happened. Like Davey, I was real fortunate to get around the big wreck."

Said Bodine, who passed Kulwicki for position with two laps to go: "After Michael fell out I thought me and Alan could draft back up there to catch Davey and Morgan. But we just couldn't do it. My car was perfect at the end. This was a great run

Grand Marshal Richard Petty, Pontiac mounted, leads the Pontiac pace car down pit row. Photographers, foreground, bow low, not in homage to King Richard, but to capture an exciting angle.

FAST START...
Ray Pinion, Executive Vice President, First Brands Corporation, gets the field off swiftly and surely as honorary starter of the '92 Daytona 500 by STP.

for me and the Bud Moore team, just hooking up this season."

Kulwicki responded, "It was a good comeback after having our best car knocked out in a crash in the 125-mile qualifying race Thursday. I really thought we had third place, but Geoff got under me. I wish I could have stayed there, but it wasn't worth wrecking the car at that point."

Trickle, understandably, expressed elation with this run.

"We're super happy," said the veteran who has been in several rides the past few months. "This really helps because we're looking for a sponsor."

Davey's understandably proud dad, third on the all-time Winston Cup victory list, accompanied his son to the press box for the winner's interview.

"I feel really good because Davey is the best youngster out there," said the elder Allison. "I

don't remember our 1-2 finish in '88 (because of head injuries suffered in a crash later that season that apparently have ended his driving career). But I saw this and I'm happy 'cause Davey has paid his dues from day one as a youngster out to learn about racing. It's a great day."

Said Davey: "Winning this race has been a goal of mine since I watched my dad do it. This is the best win I ever had."

Derrike Cope, the '90 Daytona 500 winner in the Purolator Chevrolet, strongly resists an attempted pass by Phil Parsons.

Kerry Teague in the smoking Team USA Oldsmobile (right) was through before midpoint. Rick Wilson in the SNICKERS Ford soldiered on to a 23rd place finish.

TANGLE AT THE TOP...
The big bang on lap 92, and some of the unhappy participants.

FREE AND CLEAR…
Davey Allison avoided the leaders' big crash on lap 92, held off all challengers for his first Daytona 500 by STP win.

Dale Earnhardt

FOUR OF THE

Morgan Shepherd

Sterling Marlin

FASTEST

Ernie Irvan

Ron McQueeney

ADVANTAGE ALLISON...
At the end Davey Allison had a two car length advantage over Morgan Shepherd worth more than $80,000 in prize money and untold thousands in fringe benefits.

DAYTONA 500 BY STP

Daytona International Speedway
Daytona Beach, Florida—2.5 Mile High-Banked, Asphalt Speedway
February 16, 1992—500 M—200 L—Purse $2,303,996

FIN POS	STR POS	CAR NO	DRIVER	TEAM	LAPS	WINSTON CUP POINTS	BONUS POINTS	TOTAL MONEY WON	STATUS
1	6	28	DAVEY ALLISON	Havoline Ford	200	185*	10	$244,050	Running
2	4	21	MORGAN SHEPHERD	Citgo Ford	200	175*	5	161,300	Running
3	16	15	GEOFF BODINE	Motorcraft Ford	200	165		116,250	Running
4	41	7	ALAN KULWICKI	Hooters Ford	200	160		87,500	Running
5	28	75	DICK TRICKLE	RahMoc Racing Oldsmobile	200	155		78,800	Running
6	33	42	KYLE PETTY	Mello Yello Pontiac	199	150		67,700	Running
7	34	94	TERRY LABONTE	Sunoco Chevrolet	199	146		58,575	Running
8	40	55	TED MUSGRAVE	Jasper Engines Chevrolet	199	142		52,750	Running
9	3	3	DALE EARNHARDT	GM Goodwrench Chevrolet	199	138		87,000	Running
10	19	9	PHIL PARSONS	Melling Performance Ford	199	134		49,150	Running
11	24	47	BUDDY BAKER	Close Racing Oldsmobile	199	130		38,275	Running
12	11	33	HARRY GANT	Skoal Bandit Oldsmobile	199	127		51,100	Running
13	13	1	RICK MAST	Skoal Classic Oldsmobile	199	124		40,355	Running
14	9	41	GREG SACKS	Kellogg's Chevrolet	199	121		36,790	Running
15	37	16	WALLY DALLENBACH, JR.	Keystone Ford	198	118		29,700	Running
16	32	43	RICHARD PETTY	STP Pontiac	198	115		32,530	Running
17	25	73	PHIL BARKDOLL	X1R Oldsmobile	198	112		27,960	Running
18	10	30	MICHAEL WALTRIP	Pennzoil Pontiac	197	114*	5	37,140	Running
19	31	90	DORSEY SCHROEDER	Whistler Radar Ford	196	106		25,750	Running
20	23	71	DAVE MARCIS	Abilene Boots Chevrolet	195	103		26,210	Running
21	39	14	A.J. FOYT	Copenhagen Oldsmobile	195	100		23,055	Running
22	30	49	STANLEY SMITH	Ameritron Batteries Chevrolet	195	97		24,150	Running
23	38	8	RICK WILSON	Snickers Ford	195	94		24,045	Running
24	42	12	HUT STRICKLIN	Raybestos Chevrolet	188	91		27,740	Running
25	27	0	DELMA COWART	Master's Economy Inn Ford	188	88		23,285	Running
26	12	17	DARRELL WALTRIP	Western Auto Chevrolet	180	90*	5	33,580	Running
27	2	11	BILL ELLIOTT	Budweiser Ford	178	87*	5	60,255	Running
28	7	4	ERNIE IRVAN	Kodak Film Chevrolet	166	79		43,370	Handling
29	5	6	MARK MARTIN	Valvoline Ford	162	76		49,675	Running
30	29	77	MIKE POTTER	Kenova Construction Chevrolet	151	73		21,710	Fuel Pump
31	17	2	RUSTY WALLACE	Miller Genuine Draft Pontiac	150	70		30,455	Running
32	22	68	BOBBY HAMILTON	Country Time Oldsmobile	125	67		27,350	Piston
33	21	03	KERRY TEAGUE	Team USA Oldsmobile	122	64		22,445	Accident
34	20	10	DERRIKE COPE	Purolator Chevrolet	120	61		23,115	Radiator
35	1	22	STERLING MARLIN	Maxwell House Coffee Ford	91	63*	5	34,435	Accident
36	35	18	DALE JARRETT	Interstate Batteries Chevrolet	91	55		19,780	Accident
37	15	25	KEN SCHRADER	Kodiak Chevrolet	91	57*	5	30,500	Accident
38	26	31	BOBBY HILLIN, JR.	Team Ireland Chevrolet	91	49		20,370	Accident
39	14	66	CHAD LITTLE	TropArtic Ford	90	46		22,760	Accident
40	8	5	RICKY RUDD	Tide Chevrolet	79	43		34,350	Cylinder Head
41	18	26	BRETT BODINE	Quaker State Ford	13	40		25,150	Distributor
42	36	95	BOB SCHACHT	Shoney's Oldsmobile	7	37		18,250	Engine

*Includes race leader/most laps bonus.

TIME OF RACE: 3 hours, 7 minutes, 12 seconds **AVERAGE SPEED:** 160.256 mph **MARGIN OF VICTORY:** 2 Car Lengths
BUSCH POLE AWARD: Sterling Marlin, Maxwell House Coffee Ford, 192.213 mph (46.823 seconds)
BUSCH BEER FASTEST SECOND ROUND QUALIFIER: Harry Gant, Skoal Bandit Oldsmobile
GILLETTE HALFWAY CHALLENGE AWARD: Davey Allison, Havoline Ford
TRUE VALUE HARD CHARGER AWARD: Davey Allison, Havoline Ford (M. Shepherd, S. Marlin, B. Elliott, M. Waltrip)
GATORADE CIRCLE OF CHAMPIONS AWARD: Davey Allison, Havoline Ford
MICHIGAN/MC CORD ENGINE BUILDER OF THE RACE: Robert Yates, Havoline Ford
PLASTI-KOTE WINNING FINISH AWARD: Larry McReynolds, Havoline Ford
WESTERN AUTO MECHANIC OF THE RACE: Larry McReynolds, Havoline Ford
BUDGET TEAM SERVICE AWARD: Robert Yates Racing
GOODY'S HEADACHE AWARD: Sterling Marlin, Maxwell House Coffee Ford
CAUTION FLAGS: 4 for 22 laps (84-89, 93-99, 145-149, 167-170)
LAP LEADERS: Sterling Marlin 1-5, Bill Elliott 6-19, Marlin 20-47, Elliott 48, Darrell Waltrip 49, Ken Schrader 50-55, Davey Allison 56-83, Elliott 84-91, Allison 92, Morgan Shepherd 93-97, Allison 98-144, Shepherd 145, Allison 146-166, Shepherd 167, Michael Waltrip 168-170, Allison 171-200, 15 lead changes among 7 drivers.

TOP 10 WINSTON CUP POINTS (WINS)

1-Davey Allison	185	(1)
2-Morgan Shepherd	175	(0)
3-Geoff Bodine	165	(0)
4-Alan Kulwicki	160	(0)
5-Dick Trickle	155	(0)
6-Kyle Petty	150	(0)
7-Terry Labonte	146	(0)
8-Ted Musgrave	142	(0)
9-Dale Earnhardt	138	(0)
10-Phil Parsons	134	(0)

BUSCH POLE AWARD STANDINGS
Sterling Marlin ... 1

PLASTI-KOTE QUALITY FINISH AWARD

Larry McReynolds	(28)	1.00
Leonard Wood	(21)	2.00
Paul Andrews	(7)	4.00
Bob Rahilly	(75)	5.00
Buddy Parrott	(55)	8.00

UNOCAL 76 POINT FUND STANDINGS

Alan Kulwicki	160
Dick Trickle	155
Kyle Petty	150
Ted Musgrave	142
Dale Earnhardt	138

SEARS DIEHARD RACER (MILES COMPLETED)

Dick Trickle	500.00
9 Drivers Tried	497.50

NASCAR WINSTON CUP ROOKIE OF THE YEAR

Kerry Teague	11
Bob Schacht	10

MANUFACTURERS CHAMPIONSHIP

	POINTS	WINS
Ford	9	1
Oldsmobile	6	0
Pontiac	4	0
Chevrolet	3	0

MICHIGAN/MC CORD ENGINE BUILDERS OF THE YEAR

Robert Yates	(28)	15
Tommy Turner	(21)	14
Darryl Moore	(15)	13
Ron Viccaro	(7)	12
Dick Rahilly	(75)	11

TRUE VALUE HARD CHARGER

Davey Allison	2085
Morgan Shepherd	1117
Sterling Marlin	890
Bill Elliott	792
Michael Waltrip	685

GATORADE CIRCLE OF CHAMPIONS
Davey Allison

WESTERN AUTO MECHANIC OF THE YEAR

Leonard Wood	(21)	29
Larry McReynolds	(28)	27
Kirk Shelmerdine	(3)	25
Richard Jackson	(1)	24
Bob Rahilly	(75)	23

BUDGET TEAM SERVICE AWARD

Robert Yates Racing	(28)	185
Wood Brothers Racing	(21)	175
Bud Moore Engineering	(15)	165
Alan Kulwicki Racing	(7)	160
RahMoc Racing	(75)	155

WEIGHTY TASK…
Winner Davey Allison gets an assist from First Brands Chairman and CEO Al Dudley as he holds aloft the handsome but heavy trophy emblematic of victory in the Daytona 500 by STP. First Brands Vice President Rick Bowen, left, provides encouragement to the pair. Somewhat easier to lift were checks totalling $244,050 representing Allison's total winnings.

Linda McQueeney

MAJOR MOVE...
Alan Kulwicki in the Hooters Ford started 41st and next to last, moved up to fourth place at the finish.

DICING DUO...
Rusty Wallace aboard the Miller Chevrolet and Ricky Rudd in the Tide Chevrolet dueled in the early stages.

Linda McQueeney

Linda McQueeney

WINNING COMBINATION…
Car owner Robert Yates put together the team that prepared Davey Allison's Daytona 500 by STP winning Ford.

MULTI-FACETED…
Jack Roush fielded competitive cars in the Rolex 24 at Daytona…and the Daytona 500.

Steve Swope

Ron McQueeney

WELCOME TO WINSTON CUP…
Washington Redskins coach Joe Gibbs made his debut as a Winston Cup car owner in the 500. Driver Dale Jarrett qualified Gibbs' Interstate Battery Chevrolet 35th, had moved up to 10th before being caught up in the big tangle on lap 92.

THREE OF DAYTONA'S FINEST

Linda McQueeney

Lee Petty won the first ever Daytona 500 in 1959.

Junior Johnson won the second Daytona 500 in 1960, fielded the Sterling Marlin and Bill Elliott Fords that were the fastest qualifiers for the '92 event.

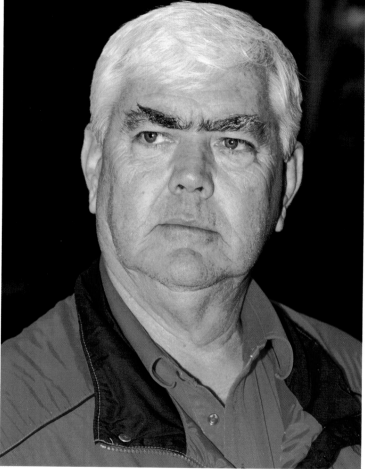

Steve Swope

Bobby Allison won three Daytona 500s, is now a car owner. Driver Hut Stricklin is a member (by marriage) of the Allison clan.

Ron McQueeney

Steve Swope

FISA President Max Mosley, head of motoracing's world governing body, was an interested Daytona 500 observer.

Dan Bianchi

DAYTONA 500 BY STP WINNING ALLISONS

By Tom Higgins

When Bobby Allison won the Daytona 500 in 1988 he was accompanied to the press box for the traditional post-race interview by his son, Davey.

That's because Davey had chased his famous father to the finish line at Daytona International Raceway as a close runnerup.

Even the most jaded members of the motorsports press corps said they'd never seen a prouder pair of drivers—nor a prouder father and son.

Unfortunately, Bobby Allison doesn't recall very much about that magic day.

It has been blocked somewhere in his memory by the injuries he suffered in a life-threatening crash on Father's Day later in 1988 at Pocono Raceway.

But the elder Allison, the 1983 Winston Cup champion and third on the all-time victory list with 84 triumphs in a storied career, said he will always remember Feb. 16, 1992.

That's the day that he got to accompany Davey to the press box as his son became a winner, too, in the Daytona 500 by STP.

"This has been a goal as long as I can remember," said Davey, the sincerity touchingly evident in his voice. "I watched my dad win this race a couple of times, and the third time he won I followed him to the finish line, just a few years ago. You know, it's hard to sit here and say this is the greatest thing that ever has happened to me, 'cause that was such a special day and I don't think anything could ever replace it. But as far as wins go, this is the best one I ever had."

Rather insensitively, someone asked Davey if winning "lifted any burden he might have felt in racing as Bobby Allison's son?"

The younger of the Alabamian's eyes flashed. "I've never had a burden on my shoulders because of my dad's name," he answered. "That's the greatest advantage a kid like me could ever ask for. To learn the things I learned from him at an early age, and then to actually get to race against him, and learn things on the race track…There's no way his name could be a burden to me. I don't want to be as good as my father. I want to be as good as Davey Allison can be and whether that's better than him or not as good, I don't think that matters, just as long as I do the best job I can every time I get in the car. That's one of the things I learned from him. He didn't measure himself up to somebody else and I'm not going to measure myself up to somebody else."

It was an eloquent reply to an awkward question. Hearing it Bobby Allison's chest expanded and his jaw jutted out with pride. "I feel very happy and very fortunate, when I think about the fathers around this country that would like to feel this way about their sons," said Bobby. His racing days likely ended by his accident, he is now a Winston Cup team owner for driver Hut Stricklin, a nephew-by-marriage to Pam Allison, the daughter of brother Donnie, another member of the famed racing clan. "To have a young guy come along like Davey…" he continued and stopped short of words to complete his sentence. Early on he talked about how he really wanted to go racing and made it his life. He paid attention and worked hard.

"He was willing to start at the bottom and work his way up. He ran the sportsman races, he ran the All Pro Series, he ran some ARCA races. He worked his way in there and earned the nice situation that he's got now. Robert Yates has a good strong team behind Davey and all those guys on the crew are concerned about him. I take a lot of pleasure in the whole thing, but especially the win today."

"I've been asked a lot since I became a car owner if Davey would ever drive for me. I would love for him to be able to do that, someday. Right now he has a wonderful deal with Robert and the Texaco people (the Yates team's sponsor) who have helped the team get where they are today. I don't think it really would be fair for me or my people to say, 'Davey, you ought to step away and do this with us.' But, who knows, down the road, what might happen?"

In taking the Daytona 500's checkered flag, Davey became only the second of the many second generation drivers to achieve the feat. The other was no less than Richard Petty, who followed his father, Lee, to Victory Lane at Daytona.

"Anytime you can match something that Richard and Lee Petty accomplished, it's a thing to be proud of," said Davey.

Now the same can be said of Davey and Bobby Allison.

DALE EARNHARDT

THE BEST DRIVER NEVER TO WIN THE DAYTONA 500

By Mike Harris

What could possibly keep Dale Earnhardt from taking his rightful place on the list of immortals in stock car racing?

The mustachioed terror from Kannapolis, N.C., has been a star practically from the moment he was turned loose in a NASCAR Winston Cup car.

Earnhardt is the only man ever to win Rookie of the Year and Winston Cup titles back-to-back (1979 and 1980).

Only Richard—the Zeus of NASCAR's immortals—has won more championships than Earnhardt's five. Since '92 is Richard's last year as an active driver and Earnhardt is just entering his 40's, Richard's seven titles is a reasonable target.

Earnhardt entered the 1992 season seventh on the all-time victory list with 52, obviously in the company of the stock car gods.

So, what's wrong with this picture?

Those six men ahead of Earnhardt on the victory list when the season began—Petty, David Pearson, Bobby Allison, Cale Yarborough, Darrell Waltrip, and Lee Petty—have something Earnhardt doesn't have—a win in the Daytona 500 by STP, the perch of the gods in stock car racing.

That list certainly is a good indication that Earnhardt is probably the best stock car driver never to have won the sport's biggest event.

And it almost seems that someone or something from above has conspired to keep Earnhardt from gaining the one precious jewel that has escaped him.

That doesn't mean he hasn't run well in NASCAR's Super Bowl.

Earnhardt finished second to Yarborough on the historic high-banked 2.5-mile oval in 1984 and has a total of seven top-five finishes in the big race.

But, while intimidating the entire circuit in recent years, winning races by the handful and taking four of the last six Winston Cup titles, Earnhardt has found some spectacular ways to lose the race he covets the most.

In 1989, Earnhardt had a solid chance to win the 500 but wound up third when Waltrip made his fuel stretch barely to the finish line to end *his* Daytona frustrations at 17 years.

The next February was the worst for Earnhardt, who so dominated the 200-lap race that taking the checkered flag seemed only a formality until the final trip around the big track.

As he drove steadily to the win that nearly everyone expected of him, Earnhardt ran over a piece of metal debris in Turn 2. By the end of the long back straightaway, he had a tire tearing into pieces and a punctured dream.

Somehow, Earnhardt kept his Chevrolet under control and managed to get to the finish line

fifth behind surprise winner Derrike Cope.

In 1991, Earnhardt was again the favorite and again appeared to have the combination to win the big race, knocking off the preliminaries like clay pigeons. This time, though, a late-race handling problem and a bumping incident three laps from the end while battling Davey Allison for second place smashed Earnhardt's hopes.

February of 1992, coming off his second straight Winston Cup title and deservedly full of confidence, Earnhardt was again one of the favorites to reach Daytona's Victory Circle.

But it wasn't to be. The Richard Childress Racing team guessed wrong on the chassis setup, Earnhardt lost a lap midway through the race and never got back into contention, finishing ninth.

"This year, we tried to focus as much as possible on the racetrack," Earnhardt said. "In past years, maybe we've had our attention going in too many directions, too many personal appearances and business things.

"I mean, we were ready for the race," he added. "It's just the way these things go. We really come down (to Daytona Beach) every year excited about trying to win the race.

"If I never win it—and I'm going to try hard to do it—I think I can handle the fact that I didn't."

Of course, it's the race you want to win, the big one in our sport."

Richard Petty, who will retire at the end of the 1992 season with seven Daytona 500 victories and seven Winston Cup titles, is sympathetic to Earnhardt's situation.

"He (Earnhardt) is maybe the best pure driver out there right now, with a lot of other real good drivers," Petty said. "Not winning the (Daytona) 500 has got to be eating away at him, because I know it would be eating me up if I had got this far and hadn't won it.

"But the thing he has to remember — and it ain't an easy thing to do when you keep having people coming up and asking when you're gonna win it or why you ain't won it yet — is that he's still got time to get that deal done. If he keeps running up front, he's bound to get it one of these days."

Waltrip, whose joy at finally winning Daytona in 1989 was almost boundless, said, "I understand what is going on there, probably better than anybody else.

"You reach the point where you just wonder what's going to go wrong the next time because you know something will. But, I think Earnhardt is like me in that he believes he's going to win every time he goes onto the racetrack.

"And, that's what you have to do, keep the faith, keep believing in yourself, being prepared, having a good team, good equipment and racing up front."

Earnhardt, whose nicknames have included "The Intimidator" and "One Tough Customer" (and some less complimentary monickers awarded by his fellow drivers) isn't about to give up trying for that prized Daytona victory.

"I'll tell you the truth, I don't want to be sitting in a rocking chair on a porch with Darrell Waltrip after we retire, listening to him tell me about how he won the Daytona 500 and I didn't," Earnhardt said. "Before it's over, I'm going to win that race."

If Bobby Allison, father of this year's Daytona 500 by STP winner is any example, Earnhardt has a whole decade to "change his luck". Allison took home his third "500" trophy at age 50.

Dan Bianchi

NOT DALE'S DAY...
Once again, it wasn't Dale Earnhardt's day. Innocently involved in the big 92nd lap crash, he had to settle
for ninth place in the 500.

Linda McQueeney

Speedway Chairman Bill France Jr. bids a fond farewell to Richard Petty driving in his last Daytona 500 by STP. Petty's record of seven victories in the classic may stand forever. He'll be back in an effort to match it as a car owner.

RICHARD PETTY'S LAST DAYTONA 500 BY STP

By Tom Higgins

Of all the emotional moments that Richard Petty's stock car racing career has produced, one of the most touching developed Feb. 16, 1992 at Daytona International Speedway.

Shortly after noon the legendary driver from little Level Cross, N.C., crawled through the window of that famous No. 43 STP Pontiac to begin his final NASCAR Winston Cup Series season, which he has designated a "Fan Appreciation Tour."

Petty, 54, didn't have to wonder when some dignitary would give the command to start engines for the Daytona 500 by STP, the sport's most important race, one which he has won a record seven times en route to an unapproachable mark of 200 victories. Petty, the first active driver ever designated as grand marshal, voiced those words himself from the cockpit.

Disappointingly, Petty spoke into that microphone from 32nd starting position in the 42-car field. An accident not of his making in a 125-mile qualifying race put him there when he had to turn to a backup car.

As he sat there Petty was busy, adjusting the safety harness… checking radio communications with his pit…going over final details with longtime team leader Dale Inman and crew chief Robbie Loomis.

Although Petty, a seven-time Winston Cup champion and likely the most popular figure in motorsports, seldom dwells

on such things, human nature dictated that in this situation he'd have flashbacks to his 31 previous Daytona 500s.

Since announcing last October 1 that the 1992 season will be his finale as a driver, Petty at various times has discussed the classic event on which he has made far more of an impact than any other competitor. Among those memories:

1976: "The one that stands out most was one I didn't win. The '76 race was the most dramatic thing you can imagine. Me and David Pearson were racin' for the win, side-by-side off Turn 4. I didn't clear him in trying to pass and we wrecked. David wound up winning, but it was still dramatic for me…I've won some 500's I shouldn't; I've lost some I shouldn't. That was one I shouldn't."

1961: "I had finished third in the '500' the previous year at age 23, and I thought I had Daytona figured out. I got brought down to earth — real literally — in the qualifying races leading up to the 500." These races then covered 100 miles instead of today's 125.

"I was in the first of the two races. Junior Johnson ran over some debris, clipped me and sent my Plymouth flying over the wall in Turn 1. It felt like being in an airplane taking off. I came down on the grass at the bottom of the banking. The car landed on its wheels, but the impact was so great it shattered the windshield. I got little pieces of glass

in my eyes. Daddy (Hall of Famer Lee Petty, a three-time Winston Cup champion and winner of the first Daytona 500 in '59) wanted me to come right back and start the second race in his car. He felt that if I didn't, I'd be scared of Daytona from then on. But the doctors had to pick the glass out of my eyes in the infield infirmary. As I came out of the infirmary there was a bad crash in Turn 4. I asked somebody who was watching from a vantage point what happened. The guy said, 'Lee Petty and Johnny Beauchamp just got tangled up, and both their cars went out of the ballpark.' I couldn't believe it. Me and daddy both getting airborne and going over the guardrail the same day. Daddy was injured awful bad. That wreck essentially ended his career."

1979: "This definitely was a '500' I shouldn't have won, but did. Donnie Allison and Cale Yarborough had cars in a class by themselves that race. On the last lap they were a full straightaway ahead of me and Darrell Waltrip and A.J. Foyt, having a heck of a race for third place. My car wasn't that good, and Darrell was on seven cylinders, so A.J. probably was the strongest of the three. All of a sudden the yellow lights started blinking. I sort of guessed what had happened, that Donnie and Cale, who had been in a bumper-to-bumper draft, had banged together and wrecked. Anyway, me and Darrell didn't lift off the accelerators.

I think A.J. did, just a little bit. Me and Darrell drafted away from A.J. some, and we put enough distance on him that he couldn't come back on us. As we came around turn 3 I saw Donnie's and Cale's cars sitting wrecked on the apron. I mirror-raced Darrell the rest of the way around, taking the low line. I gave him the outside, but I wasn't going to let him go inside me…I came back around and Cale was going at it, scufflin', with Donnie and Bobby Allison off the apron in Turn 3."

(Petty won a fight of another kind even to be in the "500" of '79, which ended a 45-race non-winning streak. Just weeks earlier, 40% of his stomach had been removed because of a peloric ulcer. Doctors advised him not to race for three months).

"They might as well have told me not to breathe. I told 'em I was going to drive and there wasn't anything they could do about it."

1981: "This '500' proved, I think, that a lot of races really are won in the pits. Bobby Allison had the strongest car (a Pontiac in which he led 117 laps). At the end of the race all the lead pack, including me, had to pit for enough gas to finish. All the others—Bobby, Buddy Baker and Dale Earnhardt—got right side tires, too (in stops requiring 15.2 to 17.4 seconds). Me and Dale Inman (Petty's cousin and long-time team leader) talked on the radio and knew we needed tires. We gambled on not changing (limiting the pit stop to 7.8 seconds). We got back on the track in front and time ran out on Bobby (who finished 3.5 seconds behind). It started as a deal of follow-the-leader in the pits, only we didn't go along."

(On pit road after the victory, the normally tough Inman wept. He had decided to depart Petty Enterprises to join another team. Inman and Petty were reunited in 1986).

Linda McQueeney

The other Petty triumphs in the Daytona 500 by STP were in 1964, '66, '71, '73 and '74.

His last victory also came at the Florida track, in the Pepsi Firecracker 400 of 1984, which was 210 races ago.

Although not winning has been deeply disappointing, Petty has handled the decline in performance with characteristic class, dignity and genuine optimism that he will go to Victory Lane again before becoming a team owner for a "hired driver" in 1993.

He has maintained an infectious sense of humor, too. For example, Petty laughed prior to the Daytona 500, flashing that dazzling smile during one special moment of recollection. "The first time we came to Daytona Speedway in '59 there really wasn't much to the place other than the track itself. No buildings or fences. They had a guardrail and some grandstands. The speedway looked as big as the state of North Carolina. It was humongous. I had seen Darlington (Raceway), but never run it. That was the biggest thing any of us ever had seen."

"The officials got all us drivers together and said, 'Hey, this is a brand new track, so we want everybody to go out and run on the flat for three or four laps.' I was 21 and I couldn't resist… I went out, stayed on the flat in the first corner and then went up on the bank. In the second corner they black-flagged me. I got black-flagged the first lap I ever ran at Daytona!"

Millions of motorsports followers would have loved to see Petty get a black flag at the conclusion of the Daytona 500—only this one would have had white checkers on it. However, it wasn't to be. He finished a respectable 16th, two laps down to winner Davey Allison, after being swept into the multi-car crash on lap 92 that set the tone for the race, and having to pit several times for repairs.

"I'm disappointed, but…" said Petty. "I was feeling really good, then there was that wreck on the backstretch and I got hit from behind. In the same circumstances, I don't think anyone could have done better than I did. I guess if I can do that well, I should feel satisfied with the race."

Too bad Petty's last Daytona 500 wasn't another great run to reflect on. His unmatched, and likely unmatchable, record earned him the right to be "in charge" at the start—but not at the finish.

Linda McQueeney

Like this one in the GLAD hospitality tent, any Richard Petty autograph session is oversubscribed, a testimonial to his unflagging good nature.

"No. 43", a faithful, well traveled GMC bus, is a familiar sight at and enroute to Daytona, sports a Richard Petty cut-out at the wheel, authentic paint scheme and racing logos.

Linda McQueeney

Daytona International Speedway

112

FIRST STP/RICHARD PETTY ACHIEVEMENT AWARD TO ANNE AND BILL FRANCE

By Don O'Reilly

The STP/Richard Petty Achievement Award will long remain a tangible symbol celebrating an era in which two families helped establish and nurture one of the world's most popular sports, Stock Car racing, and its premiere event, the Daytona 500.

First established in 1992 by First Brands, the award honors "those who have made outstanding achievements in and contributions to the Daytona 500". The occasion for the first award was a pre-race ceremony at the 1992 Daytona 500 by STP, which, coincidentally, was the start of the Richard Petty Fan Appreciation Tour by the winningest stock car race driver.

Fittingly, first to be honored were Anne B. France and William Henry Getty "Big Bill" France. Anne France had passed away, unexpectedly, just a few weeks earlier, January 2. Big Bill joined her five months later, June 7.

As is universally recognized, without Bill and Anne France there would be no Daytona 500, no Daytona International Speedway, no NASCAR as we know it today, and, indeed, major league Stock Car racing might not have reached the level of recognition and prosperity it enjoys today.

True, there was "stock car" racing back in the late 1800s as the manufacturers of the "horseless carriages" demonstrated and promoted their creations, both in Europe and the United States.

The sport gained momentum when Alexander Winton and Ransom E. Olds sat on the veranda of the Ormond Hotel in Florida and agreed to a friendly race on the beach just a few blocks to the East.

The date was 1902, the gentlemen raced their Winton Bullet and Olds Pirate to what they said was a tie, 57 miles per hour.

During the next 33 years, drivers and car builders brought their exotic machines to the hard-packed sand of Ormond Beach and Daytona Beach in quest of the world's land speed record, men such as William K. Vanderbilt, Barney Oldfield, Henry Ford, Ralph DePalma, Frank Lockhart, Ray Keech, Major Henry O.D. Segrave, and Sir Malcolm Campbell.

After Campbell drove his famed Bluebird to a new world record, 276 miles per hour, March 7, 1935, the decision was made to move the speed record attempts to the more stable surface of the Bonneville, Utah Salt Flats.

Enter Bill France. In 1934, Bill and Anne France, with young son William C. "Bill, Jr." were moving from their Washington, D.C. home to Miami. As an auto mechanic and an auto racer, it is not surprising that Bill wanted to stop at Daytona Beach and see this great beach course, site of the world land speed record and the already famed Ormond Garage, where Malcolm Campbell and others prepared their cars. Bill liked what he saw and it was many years later before the France family ever arrived in Miami, and then only for a visit.

After the family settled in Daytona Beach in 1934, France worked at Robbins Radiator Works, then at J. Saxton Lloyd's Buick and Cadillac dealership, then operated his own gasoline station on famed Main Street, with Anne's assistance as the bookkeeper and business guide.

With the exotic land speed record cars moved to Bonneville, the Daytona Beach and Volusia County leaders wanted to fill the publicity gap with a 75-lap, 240-mile race on a 3.2-mile beach and road course, March 8, 1936, sanctioned by the AAA Contest Board. Bill France drove a Ford V8 in that race and finished fifth. Milt Marion did better in another Ford that France built, he won.

After other racing efforts by the City and Chamber of Commerce recorded financial losses rather than profits, the public officials gave up. Bill France told them he would promote the 1937 beach race, with assistance from local businessmen. City officials were relieved and grateful.

After the World War II hiatus, when France worked in the defense industry, Bill expanded his promotional efforts to modified stock cars in the Carolinas and Virginia under the name of National Championship Stock Car Circuit, with Anne handling the point fund and prize money. Headquarters were in their home at 29 Goodall Avenue, an address which still brings smiles of memory to many who enjoyed their hospitality over the years.

With the fledgling industry in flux, Bill France called a meeting of drivers, mechanics, car owners, and promoters to consider forming an official sanctioning body. The three day meeting, which began December 14, 1947 in the Ebony Lounge atop the Streamline Hotel on Atlantic Avenue was attended by a few dozen racers from as far north as New England and as far west as Ohio. Out of this meeting was born the organization that is today's NASCAR.

Benny Kahn, sports editor for the *Daytona Beach Morning Journal* and *Evening News*, and Jimmy Quisenberry of *Speed Age* magazine constituted the press. Kahn made major contributions to stock car racing over the years and *Speed Age* magazine carried the first story about NASCAR nationally and overseas.

At first, NASCAR racing cars were the "modifieds", mostly Fords, an evolution from the days of the fabled moonshiners.

France felt the public would be interested in seeing races by automobiles such as their own, so the initial late model strictly stock car race under his guidance was conducted in 1949 at the old Charlotte Speedway in North Carolina.

Enter the Petty family into this equation. Lee Petty, Richard's father, borrowed an automobile from a neighbor and entered that race on the old three-quarter mile dirt track.

It was quickly determined that automobiles built for family highway use would not withstand the pounding of the rough dirt tracks, especially suspensions, wheels and axles, so NASCAR authorized modifications needed for safety of the drivers and spectators.

Strictly stock car racing was renamed the "Grand National" championship, which, in time, became the Winston Cup of today, a multi-million dollar sport of gigantic size.

The first NASCAR Grand National champion, 1949, was Robert "Red" Byron, Lee Petty was second, ahead of stalwart veterans Bob Flock, Bill Blair, Fonty Flock, and Curtis Turner.

Lee Petty became the first three-time Grand National champion. His cars; 1954, Chrysler; 1958, Oldsmobile; and 1959, Oldsmobile and Plymouth.

That third National Championship was jump-started for Lee Petty with the fantastic photo finish of the 1959 inaugural Daytona 500, Lee Petty came away the winner in an Oldsmobile over Iowa's Johnny Beauchamp in a Ford Thunderbird, after a day's deliberation by officials.

That same season, Richard Petty, 23, was honored as Rookie of the Year in Grand National racing. He had raced the previous year in the NASCAR convertible division.

In that same inaugural Daytona 500, young Richard Petty discovered the phenomenon of high-speed drafting where two cars, bumper-to-bumper, can run faster than either car alone. And, most importantly, how the second car can make the "slingshot" pass, pull out of the slipstream and by a quirk of aerodynamics, have momentary extra speed to slingshot past the leader. Richard did not then understand the scientific dynamics, but he recognized the situation and experimented. Soon it was commonplace at Daytona and, later, other super-speedways.

Disaster struck twice during the qualifying races which preceded the 1961 Daytona 500. On the last lap of the first race, Richard's car was involved in a tangle and the car shot up and over the guard rail and fell outside the speedway, a drop of about 40 feet.

Richard suffered no serious injuries. As he walked from the speedway care center at the time of the final lap of the second qualifier, he heard the public address announcer describe a horrendous crash. Lee Petty and Johnny Beauchamp, their cars locked together going high coming off the fourth turn, had flown over the guard rail, falling to the pavement almost at the entrance to the infield tunnel.

The two men who finished first and second in the inaugural Daytona 500, went over the guard rail, first and second, two years later. Both men were seriously injured. Lee Petty raced one more time after recovery, to satisfy himself he could do it, and Beauchamp raced some more, also, but both professional race driving careers essentially ended that February afternoon.

Lee Petty had been voted NASCAR's Most Popular Driver in annual ballots by NASCAR members so many times Bill France, with Lee's permission, took him out of the running in subsequent years.

Lee Petty, in 1959, with his Daytona 500 victory and third Grand National championship, was the country's first stock car driver/owner/mechanic to earn more than $50,000 in one year. Big money in those days!

Petty Enterprises in Level Cross, NC has grown and prospered. The Petty name is inscribed again and again in the record books. Lee Petty is still popular, his sons Richard and Maurice Petty, grandson Kyle Petty, and other family members prominent in the sport.

Richard Petty, the winningest stock car driver ever, has 200 major Grand National and Winston Cup victories, seven Daytona 500 victories, marked by heart-stopping crashes along the way. The smile is always there, the ornamental western hat and the willingness to sign autographs and talk with race fans, even though bone weary hours after a major race, will always endear him to the auto racing public. The Petty and France families and fortunes have been closely intertwined since the late

Assisted by First Brands' Rick Bowen, left, and Jim Vogrin, Richard Petty displays a rendering of the new STP/Richard Petty Achievement Award at a pre-Daytona 500 ceremony in the Speedway's infield. One of Richard's younger fans completes the picture. The 1992 Award went to Anne and Bill France.

50s, with the Daytona 500 as a focal point.

Anne B. France, known fondly to hundreds as "Miss Annie" or "Annie B" in the Southern tradition, was the stalwart wife, mentor, and hard worker who supported Big Bill and did much to foster the growth of NASCAR and Stock Car racing, a devoted mother and grandmother, and a solid friend. She supplied the financial acumen that made Daytona International Speedway a reality instead of merely a vision.

Big Bill France had the vision — and the courage to follow that vision — as he moved stock car racing from obscurity to the pinnacle of success. In spite of many obstacles and naysayers, Big Bill created the Speedway from an unlikely combination of woods, swamp and a bureaucratic jungle. It remains a lasting monument.

A few years ago, Big Bill decided it was time to slow down and turn over day-to-day operations to his sons Bill, Jr. and Jim.

Auto racing has been and, hopefully, will always be a family sport. From Daytona Beach to New York's Waldorf Astoria (where NASCAR holds its Awards Banquet), three generations of France family ladies have worked, planned, guided, and advanced the activities, Miss Annie, Betty Jane, Sharon, and Lesa.

On the Petty side, with Richard the "King", Lynda Petty is the "Queen", a lady who has been most active in the Grand National/Winston Cup racing wives organization, with its charitable work and year in and year out support to and for the racing men.

With this background, it is indeed fitting that the first STP/Richard Petty Achievement Award winners were chosen before anyone knew they were destined to leave us, Anne, a month before the award ceremony, and "Big Bill", four months later.

Don O'Reilly, a veteran motorsports writer, was a key staff member in NASCAR's early years.

115

DAYTONA 500...
THE RICHARD PETTY YEARS

A PHOTO GALLERY
SPANNING FIVE DECADES

All photos: Daytona Racing Archives Dept., Jonathan Mauk, Archivist

1959 Daytona International Speedway opened with the inaugural Daytona 500. Richard Petty was there, flashing his trademark smile and a ton of talent. He started 6th, completed 8 laps, won $100. Father Lee won the race.

1960 A third place "500" finish made Richard an instant candidate for stardom. He's shown with father Lee, Jim Rathmann, and Fireball Roberts.

1960 In his second Daytona 500, Richard led 29 laps, finished third in his trademark No. 43. **1961** Richard failed to start the 500. Both he and his father Lee crashed in the qualifying races.

1962 Runner-up and winner of $10,250, Richard was ranked as a top contender. **1963** He finished 6th and garnered a purse of $2500.

1962 Getting closer to the top, Richard led 32 laps, took down runner-up honors. Fireball Roberts, No. 22, garnered the winner's laurels.

1964 Richard's ship came home. From his no. 2 qualifying position, he took down top honors in the 500 and $33,300. The first three finishers drove Plymouths. **1965** Favored to repeat, Richard did not start. NASCAR had banned the Chrysler hemi engines in his cars.

1966 Fastest qualifier, first to finish. Richard added a second "500" title to his laurels, along with $28,150 for his bank account.

1967 Favored to repeat, Richard started second, finished eighth, good for $3750. Mario Andretti took the checker. **1968** and **1969** were consistent, eighth place both years.

1967 After winning in 1964 and 1966, Richard had a three year string of eighth place finishes starting in 1967.

1970 Low point in Richard's 500 record. He started 11th, managed only 7 laps, which equaled 39th place and $1105. Pete Hamilton in a second Petty Enterprises car won the race.

1971 His fortunes rebounding, a third Daytona 500 victory went into Richard's logbook, as did his biggest payday to date, $45,450. Polesitter A.J. Foyt finished third.

1972 Sideburns were in, but Richard was out of luck, out of victory circle, finishing 26th. A.J. Foyt succeeded him as the winner.

1973 Mustaches were in, so was Richard for a fourth Daytona 500 win, this one from a seventh starting position. The winner's check weighed in at $33,500.

1974 Clean shaven and smiling, Richard made it two in a row in the 500. He started in second position, took home $34,100.

1975 The signature sunglasses appear, but to no avail, Richard finished seventh for a $9450 payout.

1976 Close but not quite, a runner-up finish for Richard, from a sixth place starting slot. The payout was $37,750. **1977** was an off year, 26th place and $9450 from 3rd at the start.

1978 A distinctly non-vintage year for Richard, the 33rd finisher.

1979 Fortune smiles, despite a 13th place starting slot. Daytona 500 victory number 6 for Richard becomes history. The winning purse, $73,900.

1980 Wearing son Kyle's jacket didn't help. Richard finished 25th from a strong second row starting position.

1981 The signature straw hat did help. Richard's seventh Daytona 500 win landed in the books, a mark likely to stand forever. The $90,575 in the winner's purse would soon be eclipsed.

1982 Richard made the switch to Pontiac, which lasted through his final Daytona 500 by STP outing in '92.

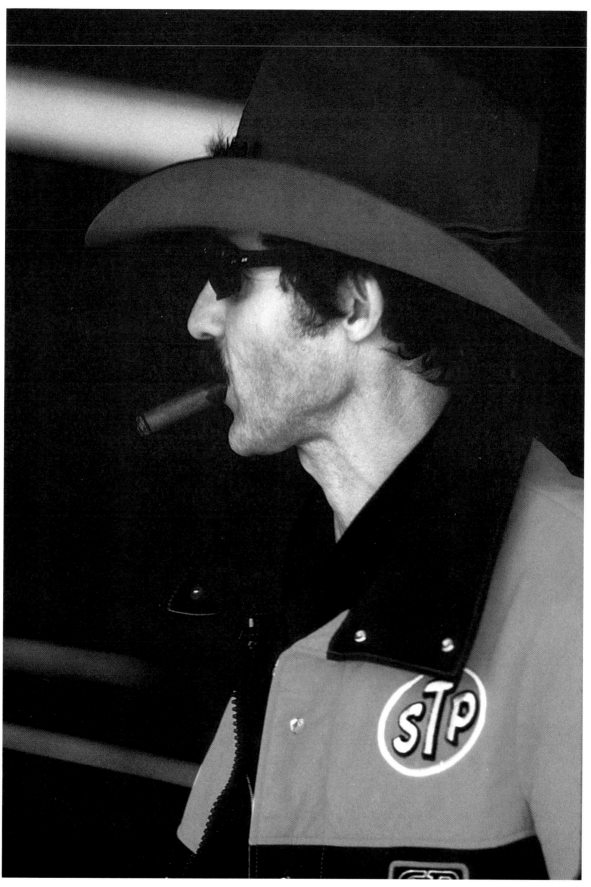

1982 The signature hat now appears in felt as well as straw. A cigar has been added. Richard finished 27th. **1983** was no better, 38th at the finish, although the $22,600 payout was an improvement. **1984** Richard finished 31st. **1985** saw no improvement in his fortunes, 34th place.

1987 Third place and $76,040 for Pontiac mounted Richard.

1986 Richard posted 36th place. **1987** saw an inspiring 3rd place finish. **1988** retrogressed to 34th place. **1989** improved to 17th place. **1990** went back to 34th place. **1991** moved up to 19th place after a rousing third place qualifying effort. **1992** In his finale at Daytona Richard came home 16th, after leading the field out on the course as the first-ever participating driver to act as the race's Grand Marshal.

Linda McQueeney

GEOFF BODINE MAKES FIRST OUTING FOR NEW TEAM A WINNING ONE

By Tom Higgins

Geoff Bodine figured the law of averages favored him winning the Busch Clash special event at Daytona International Speedway. He had been too close too often not to prevail some year.

He figured right. '92 was his year to top the rich 50-mile sprint for the previous year's Busch pole winners. Bodine, making his first start for the Bud Moore Engineering team of Spartanburg, SC, dramatically outdueled Ernie Irvan and Mark Martin on the last of the 20 laps in the 50-mile dash. Bodine and Martin drove Fords, runnerup Irvan a Chevrolet. Davey Allison and Alan Kulwicki completed the top

five in Fords. In taking the checkered flag, Bodine triumphed for the first time in 10 appearances in the race matching the past season's pole winners. His best previous Clash finish was second in 1987. He had been fourth a whopping five times.

"I'm really happy," a beaming Bodine said in Victory Lane at the 2.5-mile track, following the preliminary to the Daytona 500 that opens the Winston Cup season. "What a way to start off with a new team."

Bodine didn't say it, but he had to savor the outcome as especially sweet because he beat the favored Fords of Bill Elliott and

Sterling Marlin, who drive for team owner Junior Johnson. Bodine moved to Moore's team this year after Johnson failed to renew his contract in order to hire Elliott.

"It's a wonderful win for us," said NASCAR pioneer Moore, also a Clash winner for the first time in eight tries. "We're really pleased to have Geoff in our car and it's a boost for the team to start this way. It proves we're stronger than people thought."

The Clash was staged in 10 lap segments for the second straight year, with the 15 car field inverted after the first 25 miles. Marlin won the opening half and

$25,000, as 40% of the $290,000 purse was paid for that segment. He was followed by Michael Waltrip, Pontiac; Davey Allison, Ford; Brett Bodine, Ford; and Irvan.

Geoff Bodine finished 13th in the first segment, as he was forced to fall back because of tire problems. "It probably looked like I was stroking in order to start near the front in the second half," said Geoff, who had taken the green flag on the front row with his brother, Brett. "But I wasn't. I had to go to the rear. I guess a tire equalized. The car was shaking. It was almost out of control, sideways every lap. It was evil, a demon. We changed all four tires during the mandatory yellow flag break between segments, and it was still vibrating so bad the windshield shook. I came back in and got four more tires, and they made an evil car an angel." Geoff started the second half in third position behind the Pontiac of Rusty Wallace and Harry Gant's Olds. He swept ahead on Lap 3 in Turn 3 and led the rest of the way.

Martin and Irvan ran second and third starting the final lap and made their moves going down the backstretch.

"I could stay low on the track, and that was the key," said the victor, who won $39,000 overall in averaging 189.076 mph. "I'm sure if I'd drifted up any at all both Mark and Ernie would have got by me. I guess Mark went high trying to go around me up there when he couldn't make a move low and that's how Ernie slipped by him. I didn't see Ernie coming, but I don't think he had enough momentum to pass me."

Irvan indicated Bodine called it about right: "Mark was in position on the last lap....If he'd had a clean shot at passing Geoff, I'd have gone with him. Geoff went low and me and Mark stayed up high like we were going to draft by on the outside. Geoff pulled up in front of Mark, and that got Mark off the throttle. I then shot underneath Mark, because he was done then. I didn't get quite a good enough shot off Turn 4 to catch Geoff. I think I had the best handling car in the Clash, and that makes me feel good for the 500."

Said Martin: "Geoff would make a good football player, he blocks so well. I'd have done it in his position, too."

Said Marlin: "We went right to the front at the very start…But in the second 10 laps traffic got us messed up. We had to give a couple of guys breaks because this is the car we'll run in the "500" and I didn't want to chance messing it up."

Marlin finished sixth in the second segment and was runnerup in money overall, $33,000.

Noticeably missing in the proceedings was the '91 winner, Dale Earnhardt, who topped both segments despite starting dead last in the second one. He failed to win a pole in '91.

In looking to time trials 24 hours later for positions 1-2 in the 500, drivers generally predicted a pole-winning speed of 192 mph up to 194, depending on weather conditions.

"I think it'll be in the 192 range," said Allison, the pole winner last February. "If it's any faster I'll be surprised."

Allison and other Ford drivers are favored on the basis of unofficial practice speeds Friday, with Elliott, Marlin and Martin looming especially strong.

"We're going to do everything we can to sit on the pole," said Elliott. "I've got to keep an even attitude about things and not get too down if we don't."

Further clockings Monday and Tuesday help determine the lineups for the Gatorade twin 125-mile qualifying races Thursday that set positions 3-30. The remaining 10 starting spots are based on time trial performances.

1992 BUSCH CLASH—FIRST 10 LAP SEGMENT
February 8, 1992
OFFICIAL RESULTS

FIN POS	STR POS	CAR NO.	DRIVER	TEAM/CAR	LAPS	MONEY	STATUS
1	10	22	STERLING MARLIN	Maxwell House Coffee Ford	10	$25,000	Running
2	6	30	MICHAEL WALTRIP	Pennzoil Pontiac	10	17,500	Running
3	15	28	DAVEY ALLISON	Havoline Ford	10	12,500	Running
4	1	26	BRETT BODINE	Quaker State Ford	10	9,000	Running
5	14	4	ERNIE IRVAN	Kodak Film Chevrolet	10	7,000	Running
6	7	94	TERRY LABONTE	Sunoco Chevrolet	10	6,000	Running
7	5	5	RICKY RUDD	Tide Chevrolet	10	5,500	Running
8	12	42	KYLE PETTY	Mello Yello Pontiac	10	5,000	Running
9	9	7	ALAN KULWICKI	Hooters Ford	10	4,500	Running
10	4	11	BILL ELLIOTT	Budweiser Ford	10	4,000	Running
11	11	66	CHAD LITTLE	TropArctic Ford	10	4,000	Running
12	13	6	MARK MARTIN	Valvoline Ford	10	4,000	Running
13	3	15	GEOFF BODINE	Motorcraft Ford	10	4,000	Running
14	8	33	HARRY GANT	Skoal Bandit Oldsmobile	10	4,000	Running
15	2	2	RUSTY WALLACE	Miller Genuine Draft Pontiac	10	4,000	Running

Linda McQueeney

FIN POS	STR POS	CAR NO.	DRIVER	TEAM/CAR	LAPS	MONEY	STATUS
1	3	15	GEOFF BODINE	Motorcraft Ford	10	$35,000	Running
2	11	4	ERNIE IRVAN	Kodak Film Chevrolet	10	25,000	Running
3	4	6	MARK MARTIN	Valvoline Ford	10	20,000	Running
4	13	28	DAVEY ALLISON	Havoline Ford	10	17,000	Running
5	7	7	ALAN KULWICKI	Hooters Ford	10	12,000	Running
6	15	22	STERLING MARLIN	Maxwell House Coffee Ford	10	8,000	Running
7	6	11	BILL ELLIOTT	Budweiser Ford	10	7,500	Running
8	14	30	MICHAEL WALTRIP	Pennzoil Pontiac	10	7,000	Running
9	9	5	RICKY RUDD	Tide Chevrolet	10	6,500	Running
10	5	66	CHAD LITTLE	TropArtic Ford	10	6,000	Running
11	12	26	BRETT BODINE	Quaker State Ford	10	6,000	Running
12	8	42	KYLE PETTY	Mello Yello Pontiac	10	6,000	Running
13	10	94	TERRY LABONTE	Sunoco Chevrolet	10	6,000	Running
14	1	2	RUSTY WALLACE	Miller Genuine Draft Pontiac	10	6,000	Running
15	2	33	HARRY GANT	Skoal Bandit Oldsmobile	10	6,000	Running

TIME OF RACE: 00:15:52
AVERAGE SPEED: 189.076 mph

MARGIN OF VICTORY: 1 car length
LEAD CHANGES: 3 lead changes, 4 drivers

Steve Swope

TRUE VALUE DODGE INTERNATIONAL RACE OF CHAMPIONS IROC XVI

Linda McQueeney

EARNHARDT EDGES RUDD AND GANT IN A BLANKET FINISH

When the cars are equal, as the IROC series' carefully prepared Dodge Daytonas are, and the track is Daytona, Dale Earnhardt makes the difference. At the finish of the '92 series opener, that difference was half a car length over Ricky Rudd and Harry Gant. This pair was so close together in a rousing seven car finish that neither eyesight nor electronics could separate them. They were awarded second place jointly. There were 18 lead changes among 5 drivers but Earnhardt was out in front on the first — and the all important final lap. For his brilliance he was awarded 24 points in the

$670,000 series and last starting place for the second round at Talladega Superspeedway. IndyCar driver Scott Pruett, the surprise '91 winner of this event, had an abrupt turn of luck. He finished dead last after a cockpit fire that required some fast bail out action. IMSA driver Pete Halsmer had the misfortune to be right behind the slowing Pruett car and tagged him. IndyCar driver Arie Luyendyk had the fans out of their seats with a near spin that took him down into the infield. He managed to stay out of both walls but finished far down the field in 10th. Davey Allison, who led earlier in the

proceedings, Hurley Haywood, Al Unser Jr., and Geoff Brabham took the checker in that order, just behind the lead trio. It was IMSA driver Haywood's third IROC and he liked it, calling the race prepared Dodge Daytonas "terrific". To no one's surprise, the NASCAR driving contingent, with its greater exposure to the fine points of drafting, dominated the competition with a sparkling display of aerodynamically assisted racing. As Earnhardt put it, "I'll draft with anybody who wants to go fast." "Right up until the finish line is in sight," he might have added, but didn't.

TRUE VALUE DODGE INTERNATIONAL RACE OF CHAMPIONS (IROC XVI)
February 14, 1992
OFFICIAL RESULTS

FIN POS	STR POS	CAR NO.	DRIVER/DODGE COLOR	LAPS	POINTS	STATUS
1	7	7	DALE EARNHARDT/Powder Blue	40	24	Running
2	11	11	RICKY RUDD/White	40	20.5*	Running
2	10	10	HARRY GANT/Red	40	15.5*	Running
4	9	9	DAVEY ALLISON/Evans Orange	40	12	Running
5	8	8	HURLEY HAYWOOD/Gold	40	10	Running
6	4	4	AL UNSER JR./Purple	40	11	Running
7	1	1	GEOFF BRABHAM/Lime Green	40	8	Running
8	2	2	RUSTY WALLACE/Medium Blue	40	7	Running
9	3	3	DAVY JONES/Orange	40	6	Running
10	12	12	ARIE LUYENDYK/Pink	40	5	Running
11	5	5	PETE HALSMER/Mint Green	32	4	Accident
12	6	6	SCOTT PRUETT/Tan	32	3	Mechanical

TIME OF RACE: 00:32:52
AVERAGE SPEED: 182.556 mph
MARGIN OF VICTORY: ½ car length
*Dead heat for 2nd place.
2nd and 3rd place points divided between two drivers.

LEAD CHANGES: 18 lead changes, 5 drivers
PRIZE MONEY: The total IROC purse of $670,000 will be paid upon conclusion of the series, based on points.
POINTS: Includes bonus points for laps led.

DALE EARNHARDT MAKES IT THREE IN A ROW

Linda McQueeney

Dale Earnhardt made it look easy, leading all but 19 of the 120 lap, 300 mile Goody's 300 for NASCAR's Busch Grand National cars. The win, in the Goodwrench Chevrolet, was his third in a row, for a total of five. It wasn't as easy as it looked. Ernie Irvan in the Kodak Film Chevrolet was glued to Earnhardt's bumper at the finish with Ward Burton in the Gwaltney's Big 8's Chevrolet a close third. Burton was the sensation of the race, since a polished performance by Earnhardt is somewhat taken for granted. For 14 laps at mid-point, he dueled the multiple Winston Cup champion on equal terms, pulling the crowd out of their seats until a caution flag ended the confrontation. Burton served notice of his serious intentions early in the race by passing Earnhardt to lead for two laps.

Earnhardt promptly repassed his less known rival to reestablish order, but Burton had made his presence known. Despite the closeness of the finish, Earnhardt's biggest threat came in the form of the race's two major accidents. Joe Nemechek, having a front running outing (he led the race for two laps in the early going), spun coming out of turn 2 and triggered a fiery accident. Chuck Bown immediately tagged Nemecheck's Texas Pete Chevrolet. Tom Peck, Bobby Labonte, Todd Bodine, Tommy Houston, Michael Waltrip, the polesitter, Mike Wallace, and Ricky Craven became unavoidably involved. Nemecheck's broken ankle and burns were the most serious injuries in a tangle of major proportions.

An earlier crash at the same site, involving fewer cars, sent

Robert Huffman to the hospital with burns, put Dave Rezendes out of the race as well. Happily for Earnhardt, he was far enough from both accidents to avoid any immediate consequences. Jimmy Spencer and Robert Pressley completed the top five. While far from a runaway, no other driver was able to make a serious passing attempt on Earnhardt in his final 41 laps in the lead. The slim .22 second margin of victory was another glowing testimonial to the skill and determination of a NASCAR driver second to none in driving and tactical skills. So was the fact that it was his third win in three Speed Weeks outings, the IROC race, and one of the Gatorade Twin 125s having fallen to Earnhardt earlier.

GOODY'S 300 NASCAR BUSCH GRAND NATIONAL SERIES RACE
February 15, 1992
OFFICIAL RESULTS

FIN POS	STR POS	CAR NO.	DRIVER	TEAM/CAR	LAPS	POINTS	MONEY	STATUS
1	4	3	DALE EARNHARDT	GM Goodwrench Chevrolet	120	180	$38,068	Running
2	9	4	ERNIE IRVAN	Kodak Film Chevrolet	120	170	26,768	Running
3	6	27	WARD BURTON	Gwaltney's Big 8's Chevrolet	120	165	35,607	Running
4	17	45	JIMMY SPENCER	Moly Black Gold Chevrolet	120	160	14,300	Running
5	25	59	ROBERT PRESSLEY	Alliance Training Ctrs. Oldsmobile	120	155	27,782	Running
6	15	0	RICK MAST	Skoal Classic Oldsmobile	120	150	10,400	Running
7	36	60	MARK MARTIN	Winn-Dixie Ford	120	146	8,650	Running
8	5	17	DARRELL WALTRIP	Western Auto Chevrolet	120	142	8,000	Running
9	11	15	KEN SCHRADER	AC Delco Chevrolet	120	138	8,218	Running
10	16	31	STEVE GRISSOM	Roddenbery's Foods Oldsmobile	120	134	19,007	Running
11	8	11	BILL ELLIOTT	Budweiser Ford	120	130	6,300	Running
12	19	28	DAVEY ALLISON	Havoline Ford	120	127	6,000	Running
13	13	99	RICKY CRAVEN*	Dupont Chevrolet	120	124	13,100	Running
14	42	82	JEFF BARRY*	Barry Associates Oldsmobile	120	121	8,950	Running
15	31	24	TROY BEEBE	Banana Boat Ford	120	118	10,814	Running
16	3	36	KENNY WALLACE	DuraPine By Cox Pontiac	120	115	9,357	Running
17	27	22	ED BERRIER	Greased Lightning Oldsmobile	120	112	10,157	Running
18	32	16	JEFF GREEN	31-W Insulation Chevrolet	120	109	5,589	Running
19	12	48	JACK SPRAGUE	StaffAmerica Oldsmobile	119	106	4,700	Running
20	18	8	JEFF BURTON	TIC Financial Systems Oldsmobile	115	103	11,332	Running
21	37	92	HUT STRICKLIN	Stanley Tools Chevrolet	114	100	4,500	Running
22	21	75	BUTCH MILLER	Food Country USA Oldsmobile	111	97	9,157	Engine
23	44	1	JEFF GORDON	Baby Ruth Ford	102	94	8,957	Engine
24	30	34	TODD BODINE	Hungry Jack Chevrolet	101	91	9,957	Running
25	1	30	MICHAEL WALTRIP	Pennzoil Pontiac	92	88	5,518	Accident
26	41	6	TOMMY HOUSTON	Rose's Stores Oldsmobile	92	85	7,757	Running
27	34	25	JIMMY HENSLEY	Beverly Racing Oldsmobile	90	82	9,207	Accident
28	38	20	MIKE WALLACE	Daily's 1st Ade Oldsmobile	90	79	3,900	Running
29	35	91	CLIFFORD ALLISON	Mac Tools Oldsmobile	87	76	3,825	Engine
30	29	44	BOBBY LABONTE	Slim Jim Chevrolet	81	73	8,457	Accident
31	2	87	JOE NEMECHEK	Texas Pete Sauces Chevrolet	75	70	6,389	Accident
32	20	63	CHUCK BOWN	Nescafe/Nestea Pontiac	75	67	6,932	Accident
33	43	19	TOM PECK	Ott Furniture Oldsmobile	75	64	4,339	Accident
34	39	21	SHAWNA ROBINSON*	Casey's General Store Oldsmobile	67	61	3,525	Accident
35	14	9	JOE BESSEY*	Auto Palace Pontiac	66	58	4,400	Accident
36	23	09	SCOTT HERBERG	Luck's Country Foods Pontiac	48	55	3,400	Accident
37	33	39	ROBERT HUFFMAN*	Moly Black Gold Oldsmobile	31	52	3,325	Accident
38	28	79	DAVE REZENDES	Mac Tools Oldsmobile	31	49	4,907	Accident
39	7	10	STERLING MARLIN	Maxwell House Chevrolet	28	46	3,250	Clutch
40	10	72	TRACY LESLIE	Detroit Gasket Oldsmobile	27	43	4,807	Engine
41	22	01	RANDY MACDONALD*	GM Parts Pro Shop Pontiac	15	40	3,275	Accident
42	24	98	JIM BOWN	Bown Racing Chevrolet	15	37	3,225	Accident
43	40	97	MORGAN SHEPHERD	Citgo Ford	9	34	3,200	Engine
44	26	32	DALE JARRETT	Little Caesers Pizza Chevrolet	3	31	3,200	Clutch

TIME OF RACE: 02:15:55
AVERAGE SPEED: 132.434 mph
MARGIN OF VICTORY: .22 second
*Vortex Comics Rookie of the Year Candidate

CAUTION FLAGS: 7 flags for 31 laps
LEAD CHANGES: 13 lead changes, 8 drivers
*Busch Grand National North Driver

Linda McQueeney

Dale Earnhardt was escorted to victory circle in the Goody's 300 by a trio of Unocal girls sporting Earnhardt noses and eyebrows. For the "real" Earnhardt, it was his third Goody's 300 in a row.

Steve Swope

ARCA 200

JIMMY HORTON TAKES THE ARCA 200

Two out of three isn't too shabby. Those are the numbers Jimmy Horton posted in taking his second ARCA 200 in the past three years. This time he drove the Active Trucking V6 Chevrolet to a narrow victory over Bobby Bowsher in the L&S Builders Ford and Bill Venturini in the Rain-X Amoco Chevrolet. Horton outsprinted this pair on a late race restart, with only a single lap remaining. The next three places at the finish were occupied by Ben Hess in the Target Expediting Oldsmobile, Clifford Allison in the Bobby Allison Buick, and Bob Keselowski in the Mopar Performance Chrysler. The top 21 cars finished on the lead lap, a record for this event, one in which multiple car crashes have often thinned the field. Winner Horton and his team have designs on the Winston Cup series and plan a foray into stock car racing's top level of competition later this year. Interestingly, Keselowski, in his Chrysler, was one of only four drivers to lead the race, the other two, besides winner Horton, being veteran Charlie Glotzbach, the seventh place finisher, and Dale McDowell, who experienced an oil leak which dropped him back to 27th place.

Bill Venturini in the Rain-X Amoco Chevrolet, heads Bob Keselowski in the Mopar Chrysler enroute to third place at the finish.

Steve Swope

1992 ARCA SUPERCAR SERIES EVENT #1
February 8, 1992
OFFICIAL RESULTS

FIN POS	STR POS	CAR NO.	DRIVER	TEAM/CAR	LAPS	MONEY
1	4	32	JIMMY HORTON	Active Racing Chevrolet	80	Running
2	6	21	BOBBY BOWSHER	L&S Builders Ford	80	Running
3	3	25	BILL VENTURINI	Rain X-Amoco Chevrolet	80	Running
4	13	37	BEN HESS	Target Expediting Oldsmobile	80	Running
5	16	12	CLIFFORD ALLISON	Bobby Allison Buick	80	Running
6	5	29	BOB KESELOWSKI	Mopar Performance Chrysler	80	Running
7	2	28	CHARLIE GLOTZBACH	Floyd Garrett Chevrolet	80	Running
8	24	34	BOB BREVAK	Country Concert '92 Buick	80	Running
9	19	41	RITCHIE PETTY	Petty Racing Pontiac	80	Running
10	20	58	ANDY HILLENBURG	Air Orlando Chevrolet	80	Running
11	9	62	MARK THOMPSON	Henley Gray Racing Ford	80	Running
12	28	51	DAVE SIMKO	Mound Steel-Tom Company Oldsmobile	80	Running
13	1	2	LOY ALLEN JR.*	Precision Walls Ford	80	Running
14	29	30	RON BURCHETTE	Burchette Racing Chevrolet	80	Running
15	32	00	ROBBIE COWART	J.W. Exley Lumber Chevrolet	80	Running
16	33	02	FRANK KIMMEL	Indiana Steel Pontiac	80	Running
17	38	8	BOB DOTTER	Dotter & Davis Racing Chevrolet	80	Running
18	34	56	JERRY HILL	Jerry Hill Motorsports Pontiac	80	Running
19	15	22	BILLY THOMAS	Joe Miller Pontiac	80	Running
20	40	81	BILLY BIGLEY JR.	Tranzpro Transmission Oldsmobile	80	Running
21	26	77	MARK GIBSON	Atlas Copco Tools Chrysler	80	Running
22	11	85	BOBBY GERHART	Omar Landis Auctions Chevrolet	78	Running
23	23	27	T.W. TAYLOR	American Homecare Chevrolet	78	Running
24	27	97	BOB STRAIT	Bo Gibson Racing Oldsmobile	78	Running
25	37	67	BOBBY MASSEY	Johnny's Auto-Kustom Thread-CSR Buick	75	Engine
26	30	15	CRAIG RUBRIGHT	Budweiser-Eagle Snacks Oldsmobile	73	Running
27	17	33	DALE MCDOWELL	Dover Cylinder Heads Chevrolet	69	Oil Leak
28	42	43	JOE BOOHER	Booher Farms Buick	66	Running
29	8	96	ALAN PRUITT	Carolina Electrical Assoc. Ford	64	Accident
30	25	93	CHARLIE BAKER	Sundance Racing Buick	54	Ignition
31	12	13	STAN FOX	Blue Farm-VHT Buick	50	Engine
32	7	5	JEFF PURVIS	Phoenix Racing Oldsmobile	33	Engine
33	41	16	ROY PAYNE	Payne Racing Chevrolet	31	Handling
34	35	83	MIKE WREN	The Virginia Lodge Chevrolet	27	Accident
35	14	48	ANDY GENZMAN	De's LP Gas Pontiac	24	Accident
36	22	88	DAVID ELLIOTT	Jasper Engines Pontiac	24	Accident
37	10	9	MIKE DAVIS	Bob Schacht Motorsports Oldsmobile	24	Accident
38	36	44	BOB DENNY	Team Marketing Assoc. Chrysler	24	Accident
39	39	82	JEFF MCCLURE	Superior Performance Oldsmobile	17	Engine
40	31	10	GLENN BREWER	Tracey-Brewer Racing Buick	13	Engine
41	18	04	BOBBY WOODS	Las Vegas Int'l Speedway Pontiac	9	Accident
42	21	45	THAD COLEMAN	Dove Chiropractic Buick	3	Ignition

TIME OF RACE: 1:40:03
AVERAGE SPEED: 119.940 mph
MARGIN OF VICTORY: .16 second

CAUTION FLAGS: 7 flags for 35 laps
LEAD CHANGES: 8 lead changes, 4 drivers
*Talladega Pole Position Qualifier

FLORIDA 200 FOR NASCAR DASH CARS

MAXIE BUSH TAKES HIS FORD PROBE FROM THE FRONT ROW TO VICTORY CIRCLE

Daytona International Speedway

Maxie Bush put a big chunk of his net worth into the Ford Probe he drove into the winner's circle in the opening round of the NASCAR Goody's Dash series for small sedans. His gamble paid off and his bank balance rebounded after he took home the winner's $11,750 share of the purse. Bush started on the outside pole, was always in contention, took the lead for the third time on lap 77, won under caution. Hopefully, polesitter Jeff Collier, also Ford Probe mounted, had no such critical investment in his car. He lasted only 42 of the scheduled 80 laps after being stricken with engine bothers. All the other drivers in the top five, Will Hobgood, Kevin Brookshire, George Crenshaw, and Johnny Chapman were in Pontiacs, finished on the lead lap. Runner-up Hobgood, a rookie, was the best of this batch, leading on three occasions before giving way to winner Bush on lap 77.

156

FLORIDA 200 NASCAR DASH SERIES RACE
February 14, 1992
OFFICIAL RESULTS

FIN POS	STR POS	CAR NO.	DRIVER	TEAM/CAR	LAPS	MONEY	STATUS
1	2	22	MAXIE BUSH*	Bush Racing Ford	80	$11,750	Running
2	5	65	WILL HOBGOOD	Atlas Iron Works/Pro Cal Pontiac	80	7,550	Running
3	10	00	KEVIN BROOKSHIRE	WSSL Radio Pontiac	80	5,740	Running
4	3	07	GEORGE CRENSHAW	Crenshaw Motorsports Pontiac	80	4,390	Running
5	6	77	JOHNNY CHAPMAN	Douglas & Sons Trucking Pontiac	80	3,990	Running
6	21	25	LEE FARTHING	MOPAR Performance Dodge	79	3,340	Running
7	4	21	MIKE SWAIM	Watson Automotive Pontiac	79	3,090	Running
8	11	12	BILL HENNECY	Eagle 1/United Marketing Pontiac	79	2,890	Running
9	16	99	GARY MOORE	Lucas Oil Products Pontiac	79	2,690	Running
10	24	41	JOHNNY SMITH	White House Apple Juice Pontiac	79	2,490	Running
11	8	24	MICKEY YORK	Cobra Electronics Pontiac	78	2,240	Running
12	33	42	DAN PARDUS	Dave's A-1 Auto Parts/Spdway Shell Pontiac	77	2,140	Running
13	9	09	SCOTT HERBERG	Luck's Country Style Foods Pontiac	77	2,040	Running
14	26	98	LARRY SEGELEON	BEA Cable Chevrolet	77	1,940	Stalled
15	14	2	SCOTT WEAVER	Carolina Paint & Supply Chevrolet	75	1,865	Running
16	43	70	DONNY DUCHESNE	M&M Racing/Key Bros. Radiators Pontiac	75	1,765	Running
17	15	9	RODNEY ORR	Crosby Automotive Pontiac	74	1,740	Running
18	18	26	DANNY SNELL	Dublin Industrial/Waco Electric Ford	74	1,690	Running
19	22	27	DAVID PROBST	Mash Racing Pontiac	71	1,640	Running
20	37	90	JOHN NANCE	King Of The Hill Racing Ent. Ford	68	1,590	Running
21	40	16	DUELL STURGILL	Mercruiser Ford	66	1,565	Running
22	35	15	MILTON BRECHEEN	Richard Gruse Racing Chevrolet	63	1,540	Running
23	28	02	FLEET CREWS	Crews Tool & Equipment Pontiac	54	1,465	Engine
24	31	4	JOHN LEE	Cobra Electronics Pontiac	52	1,440	Valve
25	39	32	JOE FEREBEE	Sewing Machines Sales & Service Ford	52	1,390	Ignition
26	13	7	EDWARD HOWELL	Crenshaw Motorsports Pontiac	49	1,340	Engine
27	17	1	MATT HRUBY	Polaroid One Film Oldsmobile	47	1,315	Engine
28	7	71	DALE HOWDYSHELL	Howdyshell Racing Ford	47	1,290	Running
29	25	35	DON GUIGNARD	Buy American Products Pontiac	43	1,215	Overheat
30	1	23	JEFF COLLIER	Shavender Trucking/MSD Ignitions Ford	42	1,490	Engine
31	20	75	EDDIE HOLEWIAK, JR.	Cape Cod Auto Sales Pontiac	36	1,160	Engine
32	27	67	CLAUDE GWIN, JR.	Gwin Racing Chevrolet	30	1,240	Engine
33	44	76	LARRY COUNCIL	Pressey Racing Ford	30	1,115	Ignition
34	29	89	RIDGE SINK	Hooters Chevrolet	28	1,065	Engine
35	38	51	JOHNNY BALDWIN	Baldwin Auto Parts Pontiac	24	1,015	Engine
36	30	68	ERNEST WINSLOW	N. C. Pork Producers/TakTic Pontiac	21	1,010	Engine
37	12	28	MERRILL WALKER	Engineering & Manufacturing Serv. Pontiac	19	1,000	Engine
38	36	3	JOE BOOHER	Fly Inn Rest./Auto Needs Used Cars Pontiac	5	990	Oil Leak
39	34	60	JIM KERLEY	Exclusive Body Works Pontiac	5	965	Accident
40	32	5	DAN HARDY	Jagenmeister Chevrolet	4	940	Accident
41	23	10	DANNY BAGWELL	Mutek/Firepower Ignitions Ford	2	940	Engine
42	41	6	TOMMY MARTIN	Zimmer Gears/Burton & Martin Mtspts Dodge	2	940	Engine
43	42	95	RODNEY WHITE	Pennington Auto Parts Pontiac	1	940	Trans.
44	19	13	CARSON JENKINS	Sunset Carson Housing/TNT Racing Pontiac	0	940	Oil Press.

TIME OF RACE: 01:31:40
AVERAGE SPEED: 130.909 mph
MARGIN OF VICTORY: under caution

CAUTION FLAGS: 4 flags for 13 laps
LEAD CHANGES: 12 lead changes, 5 drivers
*Rookie of the Race

Maxie Bush's big gamble in the Goody's NASCAR Dash paid off in victory circle.

Jessica Waltrip meets the Exxon tiger on daddy Darrell's shoulders.

Krista and Robert Allison get an early trip to victory lane with parents Davey and Liz.